"Knock, Knock": The Kabbalah of Comedy

"KNOCK, KNOCK": THE KABBALAH OF COMEDY

The How, Why & What of Funny

ANNETTE POIZNER

Toronto

The People of the Books, Ink.

Contents

1.

The Comedy in Life

"Comedy is the art of hope."
Steve Epstein

I was sitting with Karen, intelligent, educated and in constant turmoil. I had met her a few weeks earlier. She was on the cusp of an important life decision. It was time to cut loose her chronically underemployed, problematic husband. This man, a non-starter, was failing on multiple levels. She had spent the duration of that marriage looking over his shoulder, having made what seemed like a safe but questionable choice at a very young age. There were no children. She was pretty clear about what she needed to do.

Each week she would come for her therapy session, sit on the couch, grab the tissue box and sob. Drifting into nostalgic states, she remembered hallmark moments of her marriage. There were banner moments; stuff that involved, say, co-parenting their dog.

Our sessions were ongoing eulogies for the man she was going to dump. She was very certain of what she was going to do, what she had to do, but, locked in guilt and self-pity, fear and self-doubt, she seemed to need to suffer before she could make a move. Delaying the inevitable, she would come each week and cry her eyes out. On my end, it was getting a bit much.

Then, one day, in the middle of our weekly ritual, she plucked a tissue. She goes completely silent, staring intensely at the now empty box. She seemed lost in thought. Her facial expression changed, the mask of despair now gone. What happened? She looked at me intently, then quipped, "Annette, I pay you good money for this. The Kleenex has to be free!" We roared!

Finally! Finally, she was on her way.

How is it that laughter has this capacity to catapult us out of negativity and suspend us, as if, higher up, giving us a better, clearer perspective, somehow loosening the chains? Psychiatrist Milton Erickson had a greeting card that he kept on his desk which he would hand to his depressed client. The card had a picture of the galaxy on the front, stars, the earth suspended in the distance. The card read, "When you think of the vastness of the universe, don't you feel small and insignificant?" They opened the card and read the interior: "Me neither."

Let's explore laughter. Mystically, there is more going on than meets the eye. If we understand laughter better, we can use it to move our lives forward. We can also eradicate destructive use of negative humor.

In the case of Karen, there were many laughs along the way. She made it to her destination. Throughout our process, though, she assured me of her monumental guilt. To that, I reminded her of Rudolf Dreikurs' definition of guilt – "Guilt is the expression of good intentions we never had!" Gotcha! Saved by a good sense of humor, she subsequently remarried and now has a beautiful child.

Laughter, Untapped

Laughter is an underused resource. Why? When something is used improperly, pervasively so, you know that the right use is not optimally occurring. Laughter today has fallen into the grip of the angry, the defiant and the impure.

Bob Newhart, a comedian from yesteryear, wrote in his autobiography, "being a comedian means you are anti-authority or subversive at heart." Today, that is very true. I gave up comedy improvisation classes. I simply couldn't take the gutter mentality.

"The world of comedy is all about smashing decorum and order. It is a bizarre, clandestine, intriguing and at times dangerous world. . . . Perhaps Rick Mercer summed it up best: " I just have this inborn desire to say the wrong thing."
Andrew Clark

Reclaiming Laughter

Laughter is a spiritual commodity but it needs to be redeemed. To do that, we need to explore therapeutic and psycho-spiritual applications. If you don't use something properly, it gets prostituted, compromised and trashed. That is the state of laughter today.

The first step, then: to get clarity.

What is Laughter?

Jewish mysticism teaches that everything that exists in the physical world correlates with a phenomenon in the higher realm. From that perspective we can wonder 'what is laughter?' What is the symbolic meaning of laughter or what is its conceptual root?

Rabbi Akiva Tatz, in *Living Inspired* (1993), points out that we laugh when something which was catapulting in one direction, suddenly reverses. That's what punchlines achieve. Think of this: some events that make us laugh are not even funny. Imagine the tall, dignified man with the bowler hat slipping on a banana peel and crashing down. Why is that funny? We laugh when something moves from one state to its opposite, an unexpected outcome, at that. The insertion of chaos. Analyze any joke, and you will find this dynamic at play.

Laughter, therefore, represents a process of transition and transformation that seemingly has nothing to do with humor. An example from the Bible. Abraham and Sarah, in their 90s, are told that they are going to have a son. The text tells us that Sarah laughed (Genesis 18: 12). It was preposterous that seniors could bear a child. And she knew that she did not have a womb!

Sure enough, she conceives. They called their son, *Yitzchak, a* Hebrew name which means 'will laugh'. What a transition, to be the age of grandparents and to transit, in miraculous style, into being first-time parents! *Any time there is a transition from one state to another, against all odds, under most miraculous circumstances, that is the psycho-spiritual equivalent of laughter.*

A perfect example: childbirth. The Talmud teaches that during the process of birth, "that which is open, closes and that which is closed, opens." This refers to the anatomy of the fetus which is perfectly equipped for life in utero but, when labor begins, the child's physiology begins a transformational process where it moves into a state characterized by the opposite of what it has been. In utero, the baby was equipped for that existence. By the time the child is born, he or she will be perfectly equipped to breathe and process nutrients in the way that is necessary for normal worldly existence. Parts of the body literally reverse their pattern of function.

To boot, if you were a Martian watching the birth process unfold, you would rightly assume that what is underway is death, not the opposite. There is that formula – something is heading in one direction and then snaps into the other direction, seemingly against all odds! (Tatz, 1993)

'Rags to Riches'

We have many examples in nature or in our lives where something moving definitively in one direction surprises us and catapults into an unexpected outcome. Think of a caterpillar that goes into a cocoon, 'deteriorates', and later emerges as a butterfly.

The Jewish tradition teaches that dying itself is a similar process. We read in Proverbs, "the woman of valor laughs on her last day." Rabbi Tatz asks, "why should she laugh?" She laughs because she knows that she is not going, as it seems, to nonexistence. She is transiting to a different form of existence, an opposite form of existence. From the earthly vantage point it looks like she's heading for death. From the Heavenly vantage point, she is moving into the ultimate real life. Her laughter is a metaphor for the very process she is undergoing.

"That moment of transformation of the self, that point of snapping out of a terrifying ordeal into the transcendent clarity of victory, is what life is about."
Rabbi Akiva Tatz

Laughter in the Lifecycle

In the lifecycle, we have any number of moments where the state of a person looks regressive, and, indeed, the reality is the opposite. When these moments occur, we are in the domain of death and rebirth. It is a time of transition.

If you didn't understand, you might infer from the terrible twos that this child is heading into delinquency. In fact, you are witnessing the death of infancy and the birth of what is slated, over time, to become a mature will, a strength (shaped by parents and other influences) to be used for good. Transitions happen in the teenage years, at menopause, at important moments like graduating from school and entering the workforce, when getting married, and other transitions which can leave us fraught with anxiety and even panic. These changes facilitate growth and literally trigger a type of rebirth – a transformation that takes a person to the next octave of life.

I've lived this dynamic many times but I will give you one example from my own life. You will think of many from your own. In February, 2019 I fell, broke two bones, had surgery and spent months on the couch. I didn't laugh about that!

But it was a transition because, with time on my hands, I needed a project. I decided to take on doing a summary of Jordan Peterson's book *Maps of Meaning*, specifically focusing on the first two chapters. That fall became a portal to progress and put new visions on the table. After decades away, I've taken up writing again! Since then I've published 11 books! Who saw that coming?

Hopefully when we fall, we rise up with new footing. That alchemical process where something negative transits you to somewhere new relates to the concept of laughter. What next steps have you been hoping to undertake? Which areas of your life would you like to midwife next?

Where is the Magic?

Where is the magic in life? I often reflect that contemporary society suffers from a terrible deficit of magic. Life should rightly involve interesting and magical synchronicities occurring on a regular basis. Curious reversals should routinely happen, like rags to riches. They are a necessary part of the spiritual architecture of creation.

I believe that certain books and films which deal with the magical or fantastical realm are popular specifically because we have deficiencies of the kind of magic that we are dealing with when we talk about the reversal process associated with laughter. There should be more crazy, 'against all odds' success stories. "How did that happen? What a fluke!" We should be the beneficiaries of the reversal dynamic, getting a boost from Above, and experiencing happenstances whereby seeming disasters effectively launch new fertile beginnings.

But if we will not live in a wondrous way, we will crave these otherworldly patterns in the entertainment that we watch or read. I say, let's bring that which is fantastic back into real-time! If we have this curious mechanism that we can access, if it has something to do with the interesting domain of humor and comedy, then we must take a closer look and see if there is more we can learn. Can we better understand humor and its lessons? Is there more we can unpack about this phenomenon and how it relates to the concept of reversal? We need to take a deeper look. That is the scope of this book. We will look at our topic from different angles. Let's see what we figure out, and how it helps us to move forward in life.

Self-Reflection

If you want to have more of something then you should track the times you've already experienced it. In that spirit, make a list of any times where a seeming negative result ended up unexpectedly tripping circumstances to come together and create a positive outcome. Think of times others you know have also experienced this dynamic. Is there a family legacy, in this regard? Are there stories of unusual good 'luck' that played out in surprising ways? You can also include here times when you otherwise achieved success against all odds, with many variables stacked against you. Make a list of fortuitous reversals. You can tweak your working knowledge of the hand of the Divine as it manifests in day-to-day life. The light of Kabbalah will be our guide.

With regards to the reversal concept as it plays out in the context of humor, read cartoon collections of Gary Larson, which you can find in a local library. Note how Larson plays with the theme of reversal, creating interesting reflections on day-to-day life by seeing some of our idioms or norms played out by characters in the animal kingdom. Brilliant work which is timeless and introduces our topic well!

2.

What's So Funny?

Ever play "hide and seek" with a baby? You cover your eyes. You are now hidden! The baby knows that you are masking your presence. You play with this theme of hiding, then the subsequent revelation, to the baby's delight. Now what is so funny about that?!

The child is older now. Now you have to work a little harder to get that laugh. How about a 'Knock Knock' joke? And if you tell a 'knock knock' joke, in a certain sense you are doing exactly what you did when you were hiding your face. Knock, Knock. Something is hidden and it's about to be revealed. The child responds, "who's there?" There is a request for revelation. And then you have what Immanuel Kant described as a "strained expectation" followed by a dash of chaos: the punchline.

Knock, knock.
Who's there?
Candace.
Candace who?
Candace door open or am I stuck out here?

More specifically, Kant said, "laughter is an affection arising from the sudden transformation of a strained expectation into nothing." In the joke, you're being led along a premise that there is a degree of hiddenness. Somebody is 'there' and they will reveal who they are. You are waiting for that answer. There is that strained expectation. And then the answer comes, laced with chaos. "What????" You are now disoriented and forced to think and think again. That initial expectation goes unmet. The punchline leaves you empty, on one hand, while at the same time the answer shoots you into a zone of thought where categories are blurred, meanings become slippery, words have become rubber, stretched in different directions. There is, as Kant would say, "a jostling of ideas." The child laughs.

As a person ages, the humor may get more sophisticated but the structure of many jokes will remain the same. During the quarantine, I revisited the humor I loved from yesteryear. I grew up watching the Mary Tyler Moore Show and its spinoff, Rhoda. Jewish humor, at its finest!

> Rhoda's mother, Ida, comes for a visit. Rhoda asks her: "how are ya?"
> Mother: "well, I have had a splitting headache all day and a little touch of neuralgia and this tingling sensation in my legs.
> (Pause)
> Rhoda: "So you're feeling good."
> Big laugh from the audience.
> Mother: "I can't complain."
> Bigger laugh.

Rhoda's question reaches for what is hidden. She wants to know how her mother is feeling. Mother answers and seems to be revealing the missing information. Rhoda's response defies the order and structure that we hold about wellness and the body. Rhoda gives us a dash of chaos! What???? "so you're feeling good????"

We will ultimately arrive at a new structure of reality, a new revelation. Ida is usually feeling much worse than this! A splitting headache, a touch of neuralgia and a tingling sensation in her legs is a good day! The scene carried us along thinking that we understood where we were going, thinking that we well understood all the categories of what constitutes feeling well and feeling unwell. We thought we were oriented. Then we were knocked out of that certainty.

Rhoda's led us into nothingness. We've just learned that we can't use our usual frame of reference. We've been suspended in space, disoriented from normality. We realize we don't have a frame of reference for understanding her mother. Our normal frame will not do. We have nothing. And that laughter will release pleasant hormones, raise the heart rate and create a euphoric feeling. So often we feel in life that we need something. Humor, though, doses us out a pinch of chaos, leading us to a fair amount of nothing. That's what Kant would say!

Nothing as Something

In the last chapter we came up with the concept of the reversal. If you think about it, the reversal is the following mathematical equation: $1 - 1 = 0$. Something, flipping into its polar opposite, takes you to the realm of nothingness.

Emptiness is celebrated in Eastern philosophy. Chapter 11 of the *Tao Te Ching* states:

> "Clay vessels are useful because of their unfilled capacity.
> Windows are cut in a room –
> empty spaces useful for lighting.
> The visible is useful because of the work of the invisible."

Again and again that text is going to urge us away from something towards nothing. Chapter 12 reads:

"many colors blind the eyes;
many tones deaf in the ears;
delicacies spoil the taste;
riding and hunting make the heart go wild;
hard-to-find treasures corrupt life."

We are going to see that when we frustrate our urge for something we initially sit with nothingness but it actually transits us back into the realm of something. Maybe something better.

Back to Rhoda. Rhoda has moved back to New York and she's frustrated because it's quite hard looking for a job and she's on unemployment right now. She comes in from a hard day and her sister asks her:

Brenda: "How was the line at unemployment?"
Rhoda: "Oh, they don't have lines anymore. They put in a whole new system."

Strained expectation. You're waiting to hear about the new system. You know about systems, procedures, negotiating lines and paperwork at government institutions. You're going along with Rhoda who's going to talk about something you know about. And then the reversal comes. The meaning you were anticipating never arrives. A dash of chaos! You are flipped into processing completely differently:

"Yeah." Rhoda says, "They throw coins off the roof and we dive for them."
Big laugh.

The best humor sabotages your expectation for what you thought was coming but, in the spirit of reversal, ends up giving you something else: an epiphany. An interesting commentary on the humiliation involved in the process of being out of work. You did get something, after all. But not at all what you were expecting.

You were catapulted out of logical and sequential thinking into imagery and metaphor. You were popped out of the left brain which collects and processes details and catalyzed into right brain processing, bringing you to higher meaning. You have a new sensitivity to the subjective meaning of unemployment for this particular character. And you get a bit of a tickle when you go for that ride.

People like to have their ideas jostled. They buzz out of their normal way of thinking as if popping into some sort of higher altitude, a more abstract way of looking at whatever's being discussed. A bird's eye view. From that vantage point, we can laugh at life, at ourselves, at each other. And that is therapeutic.

Understanding Transcendence

In order to make sense of the trajectory that we take when we enjoy humor, we have to get the Kabbalistic perception of reality. Reading Genesis, you are being told about a core reality that precedes creation: the unity of the Divine. In the beginning, there is only One. As creation unfolds, we are introduced to a world of multiplicity which, in its creation, obscures the Divinity which is at the crux of the creation. With every tree, with every body of water, the world becomes full of things. No wonder we are blinded by color and deafened by tones. Divinity is veiled, hidden, as we are distracted by all the particulars, all the fragmented bits. Our eyes are full but our inner eye is blinded. We cannot see the unseen root of creation. The veil of nature is too thick.

Kabbalah tells us that the Divine, the essence of goodness, hides in creation, waiting to be found. We could live life mesmerized by all the eye candy and fail to find the pattern of unity that is subtly interwoven into the fabric of our world, awaiting the notice of he or she who looks beyond distractions, searching for meaning. If the Divine did not hide, we would be blinded by the infinite light. The radiance would overwhelm us. So instead, we have this muted experience of reality. If we will look closely, mystery beckons, though, drawing us in. The nature of reality which seems concrete and set, actually embeds paradox.

In physics, we look closely at matter and with one measuring apparatus we find waves at the root of reality. Using another measuring apparatus, we find particles. Which is it? How can it be both? The Divine imprint is such that the concrete reality which seems real and defined is somehow ungraspable. There is some sort of mystery that defies our attempts to understand it. In other words, there is mystery hiding right under the surface of our concrete world. G-d hides within the contradictions, teasing us forward in our task, to find the infinite lurking below the surface of the finite.

Further, we will be given ordeals and difficulties. They may trip us into fear, doubt, anxiety, terror. We are being flipped. If we thought to live in the world and accept it at face value as a physical world of things, we will have experiences that will shake us to the core and cause us to look deeper still. We will be forced to find deeper meaning and to reach for transcendence because, after all, everything in the physical world either breaks or dies. We are in the world of things. It's a world of trees and grass and flowers and houses. But this is a temporary world, says Kabbalah. There is a hidden world predicated on unity and we are asked to reach beyond the concrete and to find the transcendent. And we are given the means to do so.

Breadcrumbs on the Path

If the world looks concrete, it's also laced with breadcrumbs that we can track; these breadcrumbs help us ascend and lead to an experience of one with the Divine. Certain phenomenon of this world are analogues of Divinity. Therefore, they can transport us to a higher place. On the other hand, because they have a root that you could call spiritual, they can be corrupted and lead us far astray. When that occurs, they become our version of Kryptonite. They can really hurt us. Let's look at some examples.

Sexuality can transport a person to a transcendent state characterized by nothing, releasing thought, context, shooting a person, as if, above it all to a pleasant state of arrival. If this powerful modality is used carefully and appropriately, it takes you to the doorstep of Divinity. In a context of a committed loving relationship predicated on trust and commitment, sexuality is a means of transcendence. Removed from a spiritual context, sexuality can be a tool of degradation.

How about wine? Alcohol is used in religious ritual. It is an important part of the Jewish Sabbath and holiday meals. Small amounts used appropriately transport a person to an elevated state. Too much alcohol used towards the wrong ends and the result is degradation of self and, potentially, other, as well.

And then we come to laughter. Sexuality and alcohol can motor that experience of transcendence that takes you to the door of nothingness, having left all worries behind, for a short time. Well, as we are discussing, 'nothing' is the usual destination of comedy. It takes us to the beyond, catapulting us exactly where we did not expect to land.

> Rhoda: "Ah, Brenda, maybe you'd like to stay and have a second cup of coffee?"
> Brenda (Rhoda's sister, who lives in the same building): "No thanks. A second cup of coffee always leads to the hard stuff, like a piece of Danish."
> Audience laughs.
> Rhoda: "But I thought we could talk a little."
> Brenda (understanding that Rhoda wants to talk): "Oh, okay. Sure."
> (pause) "Can I have a Danish?"
> Big laugh.

Brenda starts with this lofty intention to avoid temptation and then quickly and willingly dives right back into the temptation: $+1 - 1 = 0$. There we are, right at the doorstep of nothing! And, anyway, aren't we all like that, when it comes to sugar! There's the epiphany!

Again and again, our humor will play with opposites, taking us to the door of nothing:

Rhoda, about her process of visiting the unemployment insurance office: "every week when I get in that line, I kind of feel guilty, like I'm asking for a handout. By the time I reach the front of that line, I'm ready to ask for a raise!"

What is this nothing that tickles us so? Or, if misapplied, what is this phenomenon that can make someone feel like a real nothing, dumped at the door of complete abject humiliation. Indeed, we have to become masters of humor, to understand what it is, how to use it, how to master it.

Plenty of Nothing: The Healthy Use of Humor

We live our lives contending with darkness and ordeals. We said the mask of nature is thick. We cannot easily see the Divinity/ goodness that underpins creation. We are going to have to access that Divinity if we are going to unearth the meaning in our lives. Our lives are hard. We are constantly bumping up against each other. There is much suffering. Everything in the physical world will break or die. The process of entropy is unmistakable. How can we cope?

Your task is to pierce the veil and access the hidden Divinity at the root of creation. That Divinity is the infinite light that powers the world and motors us all forward in our quest for meaning and progress. Therefore, the concept of the joke takes you in one direction – the direction associated with the physical world: entropy. Everything is, after all, moving along to its ultimate demise. And you are not going to go along with that! You are going to undertake a reversal which effectively has you accessing that Divine Light – replete with hope and vision and inspiration and, like the punchline, it's going to blast you to a higher consciousness, one associated with positivity. In that moment, a reprieve from worries, you are awash with reassurance. The Mary Tyler Moore Show theme song ends with that ultimate message: "You're going to make it, after all!" Positivity will prevail. The clouds part. The shining Sun is right there, *after all*. You laugh. That laughter releases chemicals in the body, lightening you, uplifting you, popping you into the world of unity, at least for a short visit. (Rabbi Y.Y. Jacobson).

Divinity is beyond the physical world, whether particle or wave. Divinity is the paradox where something and nothing coexist, the ultimate Nothing, the primordial potential from which all emerges. Let's call that capital N 'Nothing'! He is, after all, the One who made something from nothing!

Timing

No wonder timing is such an important part of comedy. It's the pregnant pause. It's administering a little blast of . . . nothing, a necessary ingredient to bring the perfect laugh to fruition! That pause allows the audience to experience the strained expectation. They marinate in that moment of nothingness, getting prepared to blast off to the place where they least expected to land.

To repeat, laughter is an analog of Divinity. The reversal associated with the punchline relative to the first part of the joke completes the paradox that is the signature trait of Divinity. Laughter is contagious and we tend to laugh when we are with others as opposed to when we are alone. These social aspects of laughter reveal laughter's root in the world of unity. And laughter helps us transcend. It lowers blood sugar, improves circulation, releases hormones that create pleasant bodily sensations, some studies show that laughter reduces the experience of pain.

Laughter is one of the breadcrumbs on our path leading us upwards towards transcendence and Divinity. We are to live our lives as if coming through with the punchline that turns around the darkness that we perceive each day, allowing us to access the hidden light so that we can defeat negativity and transcend, despite everything around us that is broken, dying or destined to break or die (Rabbi YY Jacobson). We have to burst into a transcendent frame, deconstruct what we perceive as a world of limitation and open doors of possibility. We have to *make* magic happen. We have to pop out of the something of life – worries, minutia, legalistic thinking – moving from left brain to right brain; moving from the detail that prevails in the moment to the address of unity where all concepts find a relationship with all other concepts. We then arrive on the doorstep of nothing.

Back to Rhoda. In one episode of the Mary Tyler Moore Show, Mary has just met Peter Strauss, a single young man, when she was shopping for groceries at the supermarket. Rhoda says, "That's funny. I was just there and they were all out of him."

Why is that funny? Because you are thinking, initially, of all the things that a person can get at the supermarket. In the world of unity, though, there's a relationship between milk, eggs and single bachelors. They are all things that you could 'shop' for at the supermarket, albeit in different ways. That line blasts you into the world of unity because in the world of unity everything relates to everything though the connections they share will jostle your usual understanding of each of those objects.

Perhaps you will be playing with puns. Perhaps you will be finding commonalities between two objects that are generally so unrelated that finding this connection is almost . . . . well, funny!

Rhoda says, "One bite of Sara Lee anything and I inflate like a rubber raft!" How clever! A rubber raft inflates when you blow it up and that Sara Lee cake has the same effect on Rhoda.

Had you ever perceived a relationship between cake and a raft? When you find that relationship, you are soaring around in the stratosphere of ideas, above the concrete world of limitation, dipping a toe in the waters of creative apperception. You are following associations that are lateral, not linear. You are greasing the pathways of creative thinking, firing thoughts in ways that defy the usual neural highways that define every day thinking. You are getting out of your usual cognitive box, climbing above it, doing cartwheels and headstands. You must do all this if the message of the joke is going to land. You go up there, then, and hang out with your Creator, just for a quick visit. The feeling is pleasant, restorative, sometimes a bit of a high.

Eastern Insights

I find much overlay between ideas that come from the ancient Kabbalah and those from Eastern philosophy. Please allow me to segue, then, to the way that the Chinese might conceptualize the same ideas we are discussing. According to Chinese philosophy, before the world became differentiated, there was a point of origin, undifferentiated, from which everything would be born. Called "the Way," (the *Tao*) it is the destination to which everything will ultimately return, as well as the point of origin from which everything emerges.

The Chinese would say that the closer a thing is to that point of origin, the less differentiated, the more flexible. A sapling, then, is closer to the Way then a mature tree and in a storm we might notice that the sapling, lacking rigidity, may outlive the mature tree which potentially snaps in a bad storm. For the Chinese, our best goal is to re-create the Way, approximating it, divining it down, taking instruction from its lessons of balance and equanimity. Doing so would have you looking at any situation or conflict, trying to flexibly accommodate circumstances as opposed to taking a strong firm stance moving against circumstances. Effectively what you are doing is taking yourself back to the point of unity where everything is connected with everything else, looking for ways to make small, subtle adjustments that might shift circumstances in an interesting direction, finding interesting overlooked points of interconnection.

As Puett and Gross-Loh (2016) write, when you use Laozi's approach for dealing with a problem or situation, "you are actively reconnecting things, . . . disparate people, in new ways. These different connections you're making create a different environment. You are smoothing over the distinctions that had divided you from others." In other words, you go back to the point of origin where everything relates to everything else, you use that wider frame, find commonalities, soften the differences, find a new basis for alliance. You reach for latent possibilities for connection.

In this context, let's note that to write comedy we have to follow the same path, making connections between that which, in the differentiated world, seem quite separate. The comedy we watch, likewise, transports us to that place where everything is interrelated, helping us understand all the nuanced ways everything interconnects with and therefore impacts, everything else. It's a pleasant trip we take, we are happy to go. We leave our problems behind, and, hopefully, come back after, having lightened up in attitude and emotional baggage. We have relaxed our frame of reference. We go back to our familiar lives, refreshed.

Laughing at Yourself

Of course, transporting yourself above it all to a higher plain provides another benefit. It gets you away from the most limited frame of reference, sponsored by ego and vested interests, and provides a bird's eye view from which to view situations. A most productive use of laughter is directed at the self. We can laugh at ourselves, releasing the tendency of ego to take concerns quite so seriously.

For psychological health, we have to cultivate an identity, a root perception of self, "this is me, I'm like this." The benefit of doing so: a degree of psychological stability. Having said that, the Jewish holiday *Purim*, which has the Jews dressing up in costume, communicates a message: sometimes we need to pop out of our usual frame, be more creative, blur the boundaries of who we think we are and take on another persona, for a short time.

Rabbi Dov Ber Pinson reflects, and I paraphrase, we can be attached to a version of the self but, simultaneously, we must be able to laugh about it. In doing this, a fundamentally paradoxical task, we admit/access something infinite in the soul. Even though it feels like 'this' is who I am (the set identity that you live), there's more to me than that. In fact, arguably, the part that generates the wit, the interesting perspective, is the address of infinity within, the nothing, the meta-self beyond the day-to-day self. This is the part that lets us do somersaults relative to our adversities.

Laughter is one tool that we have to cope. Says Rabbi Pinson, "laughter frees us from our attachments and lets us be light." So often our ability to make light of something is part of how we overcome an obstacle.

Our character, Rhoda, is a great example of that! She brings her zany humor to a struggle that is very real for many women: food and weight management.

Mary: "Oh Rhoda, chocolate doesn't solve anything."
Rhoda: "No, Mare, cottage cheese solves nothing; chocolate can do it all!"

Or, in another example, she is making spaghetti and at this moment her sister walks in, on her way to a weight loss club. Brenda suggests that this is the perfect moment that Rhoda, herself, tag along and reengage with the weight loss agenda. Rhoda is incensed:

Rhoda says emphatically:

> "Come with you? To what end, Brenda? I am an ex-member! Come on – please – I don't need that club anymore. I mean I totally have my food thing under control." (Blurting out) "Damn! When is this stuff going to be ready! A person could starve!" (dawning self-recognition) "Wait a minute. Hold it. There it is, all the danger signs: excessive salivation, irritability and the Boston cream pie in my refrigerator!"

Brilliantly executed, we have the reversal before our eyes. We get a laugh but also a lesson. How to change states on a dime. How to find and access the disparity between different levels of soul, the physical and the spiritual. How to not take ourselves too seriously and how to access humility and do so with panache and wit, to boot.

I conjecture that any number of people learned from Rhoda's example. She who struggles with food gets ultimate victory if she can, as if, float above her struggle at the same moment as she lives it, quipping, accessing other vantage points, simultaneously. How to have one foot in infinity, at all times, and, in so doing, establishing a point which a person can leverage to architect change.

CS Lewis pointed out: "The smallest good act today is the capture of a strategic point from which, a few months later, you may be able to go on to victories you never dreamed of." It can be that brief moment of transcendence, accented by laughter that is contagious, which can effectively energize a person, functioning like a swing vote which takes things in a new direction. As far as nothing goes, that's quite something!

Brokering Confusion

Another way to talk about 'nothing' is to talk about the state of confusion. You go to school to acquire information so it might be counterintuitive to think that sometimes what you really need is a generous serving of confusion. Milton Erickson, the prominent psychiatrist, used to say, "Into every life some *confusion* should fall, also some enlightenment." It was important to him to note confusion first. The confusion precedes enlightenment. Enlightenment comes later.

"Confusion is the doorway to new learning."

Milton Erickson, MD

There's an Eastern story: a Westerner comes to the east to study wisdom. The teacher offers a cup of tea. He hands the teacup on a saucer and brings over the teapot and begins to pour. The cup is full now but he continues to pour. The student is puzzled, pointing out to the teacher that the cup is overflowing. The teacher says, "my point here is to show you that when you are already full, you cannot take in more." How do we divest ourselves of what we already know, letting go of our own frame, so that we can see beyond our usual perceptual limits.

We are full of what we know and what we already possess. Only if we experience emptiness, nothingness, do we have room for the new perspective to land. This idea is communicated in the Jewish calendar. As noted earlier, there is a Jewish holiday, *Purim*. Jews dress up in costumes, drink enough alcohol so they will confuse the name of the villain in the Purim story with the name of the hero. They listen to the reading of the Purim story.

A couple months later, in the spring, is Passover. The confusion of *Purim* is the prequel. You wipe out your frames, dress in a costume (explore new parameters of who you are, parameters that are very different from your normal day-to-day experience). Get drunk (confused) and so lose your normal frame of reference. Then you will be ready in the spring to read the Passover story and emerge, fresh, into a new reality characterized by transcendence.

At *Purim* you listen to the *Megillah*. You are a blank state. We want you empty. If you want to replace your wardrobe, you have to first get rid of the old stuff, then start wearing the new. You empty, fasting during the day until the evening when you go to listen to the *Purim Megillah*, at night. Then, listening, you fill yourself with the story of redemption. By spring, you will be ready to read the Passover *Haggadah* aloud. You become a mouthpiece for redemption. You're ready to speak. Confusion in late winter is the breeding ground for the clarity which unfurls in the spring!

In this light, think of humor as an opportunity to drop preconceptions, to dance with confusion and its first cousin, Nothing. Erin Bouma described 'certainty' as "a hardening of the categories." Humor, then, loosens the rigidity, blurs the categories. It's a frame which softens and shakes off the dead wood.

> Rhoda's mother is delighted that she now has both girls in the same city. She says: "it's nice to be with my two girls, Rhoda Faye, Brenda Faye."
> Audience laughs.
> Rhoda: "Ma, if you like the name Faye so much, why didn't you just name one of us Faye."
> Mother (testy): "I didn't like it that much!
> Big laugh!

Absolutely ridiculous! But now we are stretched with a new idea. We thought a person either likes a name or doesn't like a name.

Turns out they can like a name enough that they are going to use it for a middle name, even twice, but that's still not liking it enough to give one of those daughters that name as a first name. Who knew? You've just had to stretch your thinking.

The world of unity delights to have you think upside-down and sideways. Stuff you never thought of before. It wants to bend the way you think and at the same time you've just been transported to planet Nowhere. She likes the name. She doesn't like the name. $+1 - 1 = 0$. The laughter is the light, the Divinity, your Divinity, that lights up when you are brought to the realm of transcendence.

"Certainty is a portable prison."

Caroline Casey

Rhoda shows up, a surprise visit for her mother. Her mother, ever competitive, delights, then says, "Just a second. I have to make a phone call." She picks up the phone: "Hello Edna? (pause) "I was calling to invite you down for coffee but as it happened my daughter Rhoda walked in so I'm calling to cancel." (pause). "Yes. She brought me a present." $+1 - 1 = 0$.

Cracks me up every time.

Bed, Bath & Bus

Ever notice when you are prone to get some of your most fertile ideas? One scientist reflected that many in his field came up with their inventions or clarities when they were taking a bath, riding on the bus or dreaming at night. Of course there are many stories of such inventions, the most famous of which is Albert Einstein coming up with his theory of relativity in the course of dreaming. When are we most likely to land our inspirations? When our minds are wandering. What are we thinking about? Nothing!

Nothing is the purveyor of something. We are usually so full of our everyday lives and busyness, it's not so easy to find the path to emptiness and nothingness. Laughing is one way.

Another way, though, is through the use of hypnosis. If you study the language of hypnosis, the language that sends people into a transcendent state, don't be surprised when you find language that follows our principle of nothing. The hypnotist may use many phrases that involve reversals: "you can look forward to looking back on . . " "Having left every worry behind, you can move right into the developing comfort." The hypnotist may make specific reference to both the conscious mind and the unconscious mind. In other words, by saying, "your conscious mind can think and analyze while your unconscious mind can explore the developing comfort," you are capturing the two polar opposites of selfhood, the conscious and the unconscious. When you speak to both of them and describe each of them simultaneously, you are zoning a client into that experience of nothingness, the place of unity where all the opposing fragments of self come together as a unified whole.

The very language of hypnosis is the language that promotes transcendence. Any time you run somebody from one facet to the opposite facet, whether by architecting a joke, doing a hypnotic induction, creating a work of art with those themes shining out, you are moving your listener or viewer towards transcendence, the place where opposites meet. Now the question is, when you get up there, who's there with you?

'Who' *is* There

"Knock, knock." "Who's there?"

It's interesting. In Hebrew the word for 'who' is *mi*, pronounced me. In Hebrew, every Hebrew letter has a number associated with it and therefore every word has a sort of numerology. So this particular Hebrew word, *mi*, has a numerical value of 50. And 50 is the number associated with transcendence. You know who is the ultimate who? That word, *mi*, is one of the names of Divinity. Why? Because G-d is the Who at the root of creation. At the end of the day, he's the only one here. We are all fragments, comprised of and motored by the light of the Divine.

There it is: knock knock. Who's there? Read that as a statement. Who is there! Sounds like a comedy routine, I know. But, as we've mentioned already, the punchline is always and only about some sort of revelation of the Divinity, the world of unity, that exists beyond mundane life. We are all reaching for the ultimate access to *Who*, the One we can't see, the One with whom we will delight when we finally meet up after a life well-lived. He's your Number 1!

"Who can light the world up with her smile?"

Speaking of who, I'm mentioning the Mary Tyler Moore Show throughout this book because there is a lot to unpack about that show. Now when you look at that theme song, of course you're going to find all our key themes. "Who can take a nothing day, and suddenly make it all feel worthwhile." We have our reversal, from nothing to something. We have our nothing which gives way to transcendence, something much better. And we even have the ultimate Who at the root of creation. So don't hear that lyric as a question! Here it as an answer: *Who* can take a nothing day and suddenly make it all feel worthwhile. Yup. That's what Divinity can do.

As an interesting aside, when the producers of that show were looking for a theme song, someone brought them this one to consider. They both lit up! "This is it!!" Immediate recognition that this was the lyrics they needed, this was the melody they were looking for. I find that interesting . . .

In the introduction we looked at the whole theme of reversal. Now, we've been getting a little clearer on what's happening when we go for the ride and reverse, zooming ourselves out of the world of physicality, the mundane world, and shooting ourselves into a much more ephemeral sphere. Perhaps we are en route to what Emerson described when he wrote the following:

> Standing on the bare ground – my head bathed by the blithe air and uplifted into infinite space – all mean egotism banishes. I become a transparent eyeball; I am nothing; I see all; the currents of the Universal Being circulate through me; I am part or parcel of G-d."

Yes. Our Divinity expresses itself through a state of nothingness. That state of laughter, that surrender where a person is enveloped with the kind of ticklish response to what they are seeing or hearing, is a brief encounter with the infinite. It doesn't last long but it gives us a whiff of something beyond our current existence.

In the next chapter, I'd like to detour into another sort of examination. While different people laugh differently, there is something common about how many people laugh and we see it when we note how laughter is represented in literary composition. You might read about Santa's "ho ho ho." Or maybe rendered in emails as "ha ha ha." You might notice a few "hee, hee"s or "heh!" Note the commonality: in English it would be the letter *H*. Believe it or not, looking at the raw sound of laughter is going to take us somewhere interesting that advances our analysis.

Exercises

Attend a drop-in improvisation class or sign up for a series of classes. Get used to thinking out of the box and letting your mind take you in all directions. We need to limber up and encourage cognitive flexibility. Do creativity exercises. Play Sudoku. Pay the low monthly fee for Brain HQ, a software program comprised of brain exercises that improve cognitive processing skills, so you can cultivate more cognitive flexibility.

Why all this?

As Gandhi said, "be the change you want to see in the world!" Change your patterns of thinking. Get funnier. Learn jokes and tell them. Court the energy of reversal. Funny things happen to funny people.

Stop watching so much TV and take up writing. By hand. The pen is a magic wand.

If you watch TV to relax, watch old Rhoda reruns on YouTube. That series, very well written, has you watching characters contend with ordeals by using humor and language play to cope and transcend.

Read about the late psychiatrist Dr. Milton H Erickson, a veritable magician. Read Jay Haley's book about him called *Uncommon Therapy: The Psychiatric Techniques of Milton H Erickson*. Get ready to laugh! Erickson had his own way of setting up reversals, called paradoxical therapy, to help tip people into health and better psychological function.

Milton Erickson had an exercise he would assign to his students to have them learn to think in all four directions. He would encourage them to pick up a book of fiction and to read the last chapter. Once they did that, he would ask them to make a list of their guesses of what happened in the chapter that preceded the last chapter. Then they were to read that chapter and similarly make guesses: what happened in the preceding chapter? And so on and so forth. He said that reading books backwards would teach a person to think in all four directions. Try it.

Study magic. Buy tricks and show your friends. Be a living emissary of the reversal mechanism and brighten people's day!

3.

The 'Aha' of Ha Ha: Analyzing Laughter

When you look through the lens of Kabbalah, literally everything is stamped with the fingerprint of the Divine. I'm going to make a case that the sound of the letter *h,* prominent in the sound of laughter, whether we hear "ha ha," or "ho ho," "hee, hee," or some other variant, is relevant. In English we have the letter *H* but in Hebrew that letter is called the *Hey.* That letter has great mystical significance. On a functional level, it's the letter that is used to represent Divinity. If, writing Hebrew, you are taking quick notes and want to represent G-d in one letter, *Hey* is the abbreviation. G-d's representative in shorthand! Every Hebrew letter has a numerical value. The numerical value of this letter is the number five, as in the five books of Moses.

Know what the word 'quintessential' means? The first syllable in that word is the number five in Latin. Here's the idea: there is a fivefold essence of everything. Chinese medicine has "Five Element Theory." The physical world is associated with four seasons and four directions but also is infused by the fifth dimension, the Divinity, cloaked, that is, embedded in every living thing and in the world, itself. There are five mentions of the

Hebrew word, *ohr*, light, in the first lines of Genesis, representing the fivefold light at the root of creation.

You've probably heard of the Fibonacci numbers named by Leonardo of Pisa. He introduced this very special sequence of numbers to Western European mathematics. The Fibonacci numbers represent proportions that are found in the human body and are widely observed in nature. In nature, this series of numbers predicts the consistent pattern of growth of leaves as they spring from a stem, describes the rate of procreation in certain species of animals or insects and predicts the most popular number of pedals on flowers. Hundreds of flowers have five pedals. The Fibonacci numbers dictate how branches in the tree will grow. These numbers also predict those proportions that are most pleasing in artistic creation and in architecture. The formula which expresses this particular sequence of numbers can be expressed in all fives:

$$Phi = 5 \wedge .5 \times .5 + .5$$

Looking at the body, we see the way the number five is imprinted on each limb through fingers and toes and see five appendages to the torso. The mystics assert that the soul has five aspects, using five different names. Although the Divine name known as the Tetragrammaton only has four letters, Kabbalah asserts that a particular mark in the calligraphy of the first letter represents the fifth, concealed facet of the Divine. No wonder that the religious (who do not depict the name of Divinity casually), will instead handwrite the *Hey* as the signifier for the One Above who clearly has a thing for the number five.

For the Chinese, the number five represents the magnificent ecosystem of nature as it manifests in the natural world out there and the one "in here," in the human body. Five Element Theory renders the interrelationships between earth, metal, water, fire and wood. This model describes an intriguing web of relationships wherein each element is nourished by one of the others, (for example, water nourishes wood) and each is inhibited or limited by one of the others (for example, water inhibits fire). Therefore, this theory captures the elegance of nature, including our own inner nature, governed, as it is by innumerable checks and balances woven right into the system.

Why 'Hey'?

Why does laughter bear the imprint of this particular Hebrew letter and not another? We have to look a little bit deeper into the letter to understand better.

In Hebrew, each letter has meaning. The shape of the letter is significant and relates to the concept of the letter. Each letter has a numerical value and that, too, will be meaningful and will relate back to the concept represented by the letter. The particular Hebrew letter we are discussing, pictured, is comprised of two other Hebrew letters. One is a distinctly 'feminine' letter, the other masculine. In other words, this Hebrew letter is the Jewish version of the Chinese *Tai Ji/Yin-Yang* symbol. We need to look further.

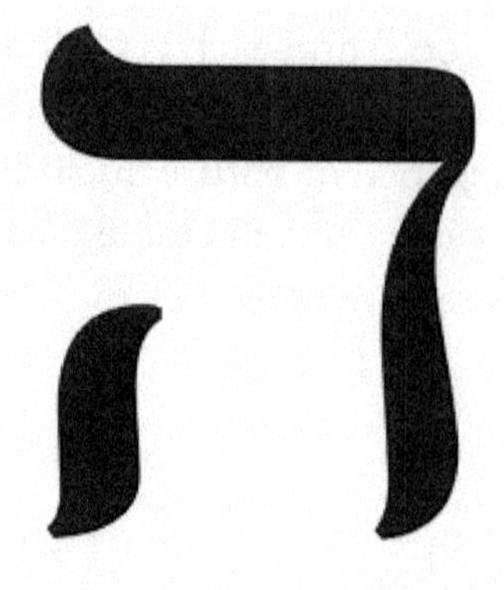

Fifth Hebrew letter: Hey

Within the *Hey*, the letter on the right is another Hebrew letter, *Dalet*, the fourth letter in the alphabet, the letter which represents the number four. The shape of the letter represents the beggar, bent over, denigrated, with a hand outstretched to the back to accept charity.

The *Dalet* represents the physical world in which everything either breaks or dies. The four associates with the four seasons and the four directions. It's no coincidence that our English words for die, dead and death use that consonant.

For the Chinese, the number four is unlucky. The Chinese word for that number sounds very much like the Chinese word for death and therefore a Chinese patient is not happy to get medical feedback in a treatment room labelled with the number four. I learned this firsthand, when my Chinese doctor had four treatment rooms and labelled them 0, 1, 2 and 3! *Dalet* associates to the physical dimension of life: Mother Earth. Hence, the feminine label. The ultimate masculinity, of course, is Divinity, eternal, everlasting. Death, then, is a state of Yin, femininity, passivity but also alludes to birth and regeneration, insofar as death releases the soul to ascend to a new level of existence.

On the lower left of our Hebrew letter *Hey* we find the masculine letter *Yod*. This is the smallest letter in the Hebrew alphabet. This is the one letter that, in its place in the Hebrew alphabet, is suspended high above the line. The rest of the Hebrew letters sit on the baseline. This letter hovers. How can we understand that letter?

With regards to its smallness: that which is spiritual always takes the minimum amount of space and time. This tiny letter is like a time-release vitamin which explodes into the Big Bang. It's this little burst of something which carries the energy of the Divinity into creation. It's the 10th letter of the Hebrew alphabet and represents the concept of perfection, associated with the number 10. It also represents the 10 Divine Attributes that mysticism associates with Divinity. This letter hovers above the line because it is other-worldly. It is above and beyond the physical.

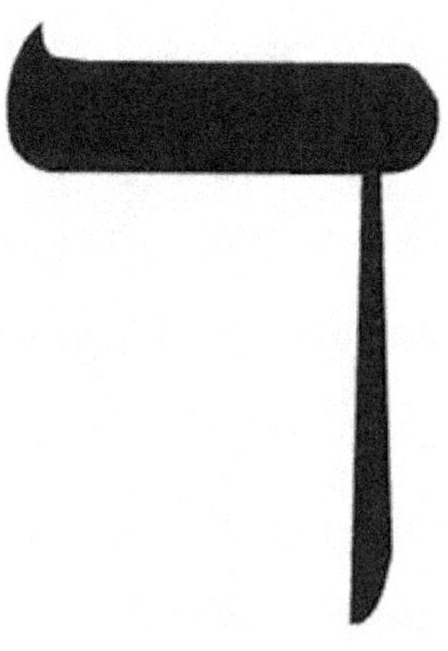

Fourth Hebrew letter: Dalet

You could think of our bodies and souls as represented by the Hebrew letter *Hey*. We have these two dimensions. Our *Yang* dimension is our Divine spark which enlivens us and drives us, catalyzing us, motivating us, brightening us, drawing us towards what we love to do. It's the brightness in our eyes. It's the love in our hearts. The feminine letter is our physical body which is eventually destined to go back to the earth. With time and age, we become bent over! We weaken! But the human endeavor is to architect these two aspects so that they inter-penetrate and are otherwise properly choreographed. The *Hey* creates the possibility for these two dimensions which are intrinsically opposite to come together! There's information in this Hebrew letter *Hey* that we do not find in the Chinese symbol of *Yin* and *Yang*.

Tenth Hebrew letter: Yod

The *Yod*, this floating letter, represents the fact that our masculinity or our Divinity prefers to be unfettered. ADHD is the living expression of this sort of energy when it is unbounded, undisciplined, when it is not properly bound to the physical.

In essence, the message when the masculine letter is yanked from its floating status and inconspicuously shoved to a lowered position within another letter: we have to grab a hold of our spiritual essence and ground it or it will drag us around and may result in an unbalanced way of living. Too much excitement and we skip meals, don't sleep properly and trash the body. Too much love and a person can be promiscuous, loving too many people. The feminine provides a structure and invites the masculine Hebrew letter to displace itself from the freedom it has when it is hovering above the line, inviting it into a structure where it has to unplug from freedom in order to actualize potential.

For example, the masculine can see potential anywhere. Imagine a young man. He sees many wonderful attractive women, perhaps each of whom would be a good partner. In order to properly move forward, developmentally speaking, he's going to have to unplug from the world of all potential to pick one woman and, so, to build something with her and let go of all the others with whom he cannot equally invest and develop relationship.

If the masculine nature is not managed, he will hover above, delay commitment and continue to identify new and more potential, never bunkering down and building something with one person. Imagine a young person who can't decide which field to go into. He's good at this. He's good at that. At a certain point, he has to start. Just pick one discipline or direction and invest. That process is akin to plucking the *Yod* from its place above the line and grounding it in a feminine structure. All this is represented in the Hebrew letter *Hey*.

And this *Hey* is the letter that we hear in a laugh: the letter that represents the proper choreography when masculine and feminine have come together in a healthy way. Again and again we are going to see that the domain of laughter takes us to the world of unity, the place where the masculine and the feminine, the something and the 'nothing', coexist in perfect harmony. We go back to the zone of pure potential, it's like going back to factory settings. From there we can come back with a fresh perspective and new inspiration. No wonder so many creative inventions are spawned from bed, bath and bus. As creative as we are, it really takes some degree of catalyzing the spark of Divinity within to really come up with the better ideas, to build a better mousetrap. Laughter is potentially one way there.

Why 'Hey' Is Just Not into You

If you recall the story of Abraham in the Torah, you may remember that his initial name was *Avrum*. He went through a series of ordeals and one of them involved circumcising himself, commanded by G-d. It was a bit of an obstacle course, many tests, then at the end he merited to have a name change. Suddenly, this Hebrew letter was added to his name and also added to his wife's name.

Let's think of *Hey* as *Qi*, the life force (as per Chinese Medicine), that comes down from above and animates us. It's an allocation of Divine light and if we prepare the vessel, we can properly integrate this light and so will be beneficiaries of energy, radiant health and also psycho-spiritual maturity. In fact, the act of coming of age is nothing less than a young person figuring out how to access this Divinity and so actualize greatness. In the Hebrew Bible, we read narratives of people who come of age. Jacob wrestles with the angel; then he has a new name, Israel. Joseph goes through his ordeals to come to fruition. And many more such stories.

In a sense, we all have to wrestle with the angel and so earn our new name. Stephen Wolinsky, a psychologist, said, "in order to become who we truly are, first we have to become who we are not." Therefore, we should take great issue with Lady Gaga's song: "Born That Way." We are all born with our imperfections, approximately made in the image of the Divine but needing to undergo a process of self-perfecting. [1] In Kabbalah, the way you are born is merely your starting point. Jordan Peterson, the psychologist, would say, "don't kill your future self." Don't let your current self crowd out the person that you could be if you brought out more potential from within. Who could you next become if you modified and improved the vessel?

How can we reach into our best potential and develop? By preparing the vessel so that we integrate as much of the energy, signified by the Hebrew letter *Hey,* as we can. This is the way that we actualize and bring down our allocation of Divinity.

There is a book that has been written for women who are trying to date more successfully: *Why He's Just Not into You.* I'd say that we are on focus if we understand that we need to make ourselves into magnets that will draw *Yang* energy towards us; off track if we think our only issue is to figure out how to attract the right mate. In my mind, the title of the just-mentioned book should better be: "Why *Hey* is Just Not into You" What is off about your lifestyle that you are not fully benefiting from the Divine influx of light

---

1. This is the topic of my book, *Reading the Soul: Kabbalah and the Psychology of Handwriting.*

that would bring you best health, best energy, best synchronicity, and help you meet the one who is your destined best partner?

Good Flow

You've likely heard the Hebrew phrase "*Mazel tov!*" Perhaps you think it means "congratulations!" Or "good luck." Wrong. *Mazel* comes from another Hebrew word *nozel*, think of the English word nozzle. *Nozel* refers to flow. This phrase that we use quite freely is a blessing where we extend the wish that others will be optimally situated so that they are the beneficiaries of Divine flow.

How do we achieve this? By calibrating our inner masculine and feminine selves, by architecting ourselves, by tweaking our imperfections, by sorting ourselves out, by taming excesses in the personality and animating or developing those attributes we have which are weak. In so doing, we are developing the vessel and becoming structures which magnetically attract an infusion of Divinity. That Divinity is coursing in us, through us and around us at every moment. It wants in! But is the vessel prepared? Now that is the question. There is a way to live so that we will be bringing more nothing/Divine light into the something of our physicality and egoic self. Living this way, we embody good flow. Work becomes easier. Synchronicities happen. You meet the people you need to meet and you get a good intuitive sense of the people around you who are not life enhancing. You move on.

Kabbalah teaches that we have two selves: an animal soul and a divine soul. Initially, as children, we are predominantly animating the animal soul. As we continue to refine ourselves, to grow, to master our energies and so become more competent beings, more and more of the Hebrew letter *Hey* and it's influx of energy is integrated into our system. The Divine soul gradually takes root. Our narcissism fades, that being the residue of the animal soul. But as we become more competent, we are characterized by the expansive energy of the Hebrew letter *Hey*. We absorb it, we shine it out into the world. Until then, we are subject to reactivity, fixation and contraction. Childishness. We have to move from our smaller self to the infinite self associated with Divinity. The Hebrew letter *Hey* beckons us. If we're not living well, it's just not into us.

Well, I think you've seen that we have just undergone a little reversal! This book is about laughter but it turns out that the fun of laughter may be a side benefit, the least important point when it comes to laughter as a phenomenon. The real message of laughter is much deeper.

Laughter wants to take us on a journey out of ourselves to the land where we've never been, to the land of our best potential. No wonder the first Jewish child born as per the account of the Torah is named *Yitzchak*, or 'he will laugh.' No wonder the majority of comedians are Jewish, as if imprinted with this task. No wonder so many people, when writing personal ads, cite a sense of humor as an essential trait for a potential partner.

We started addressing the theme of laughter but the real address of our discussion is who we are becoming and how we can become our best selves. Having said that, I'm not done with laughter. The stimulus of this book was my re-engagement with the Mary Tyler Moore Show and the spinoff, Rhoda. Forty five years later I now understand what those shows contributed to the culture, shows designed by a bunch of funny Jews in tandem with Mary Tyler Moore, herself, to help a generation navigate a difficult reversal, one cosmically ordained to occur as per the early account in Genesis. More on that next.

4.

Mary Tyler Moore's (Jewish) Legacy

Revisiting the shows that escorted me through adolescence got me thinking about Mary Tyler Moore. I poked around on YouTube. Somebody did a little film of her gravesite and, on the elaborate monument you see many small stones. If you've been to a Jewish cemetery, you know what those are. In the Jewish tradition, when visiting a cemetery, one brings a small stone and leaves it over top the grave or resting on the tombstone, a reverential sign of respect, as if you, yourself, are creating a monument to remember the deceased.

It was interesting to see all those little stones. Her third husband was Jewish and surely his friends and family would bring those rocks. But recall, so many of those who worked for her to create that show were also Jewish. Mary Tyler Moore had a strong tie to the Jewish world that helped create her legacy.

In the last chapter, we spoke of *mazel*. I'm going to suggest that the Mary Tyler Moore Show clearly had *bracha*, blessing, extended from the higher world. There was flow, Divine flow, that made that show and its offshoots unusually successful. Bear in mind, Mary had been asked to star in a sitcom. The other performers hired by Edith Winant, who did the casting, had solid resumes but had not achieved success of note. Their launch to stardom was via the MTM Show.

What's interesting: that show launched these performers, *unlike* any other show. When MASH, another popular sit-com of that day, called it quits, you did not see all those players go on to land parts in other sitcoms. With regards to the MTM Show, Valerie Harper starred in Rhoda and, then, another series. Ed Asner was Lou Grant. That show had longevity. Betty White landed in various sit-coms. Gavin MacLeod had longevity with Love Boat. Ted Knight and Cloris Leachman also had shows. How rare for all the players of a sitcom to have such success, after their sit-com ends.

For that matter, Rhoda, an MTM spinoff, launched Julie Kavner. She has become a multimillionaire for her work on the Simpsons. As an interesting bit of trivia, one of the Rhoda episodes had Brenda, played by Kavner, serving as the bank teller for Woody Allen who was supposedly banking at her branch. The show played on this idea, though Woody Allen did not appear in that episode. A few years later, once Rhoda had been cancelled, Allen used Julie Kavner for parts in several of his movies, a stepping stone in her career. This episode presaged their later work together!

Beyond what I've mentioned, there are many other ways this show was unusual. The close team ship of the company has been documented, a testimony to the friendships of all involved, not normative of TV production companies, as a rule. The fact that this show was disbanded after seven years when the ratings were high is also interesting. The writers and producers wanted to move onto new projects. There was gold in them thar' hills! This show was a springboard for many to take their talents further afield.

What is it about these MTM productions that there should be 'flow'. *mazel*, which would bear fruit for the company and the players? I'd like to suggest that the MTM Show and Rhoda, both, had Kabbalistic import. To understand better, we have to go back to Genesis.

Yin, Yang & You

We keep making our way back to revisit the polarity of the universe. We said the Chinese medical theory depicts an archetypal pattern that pervades the universe, adding a rhythmic quality to our days, our seasons and our lives. *Yin* and *Yang* debuted in Genesis when we learned of a rhythmic world of light and dark, day and night, male and female. Later, the Jews were sanctioned to make distinctions between the two polarities in all their expressions. With regards to diet, milk is prepared separately from meat. Relative to clothing, Jews do not wear a garment which has both linen and wool within it. More generally, Jews vary their rituals in accordance with the alternating cycle of night and day. Making distinctions between *Yin* and *Yang* rests at the heart of Jewish life, accounting for the first formal blessing a Jew recites every morning, an expression of appreciation for the ability to distinguish between day and night.

You could get the impression that *Yin* and *Yang* enjoy equal stature in Judaism, albeit we make distinctions between them. In fact, in Genesis, we learn this is not to be the case. In describing the process of creation, Genesis 1:16 reads, "And G-d made the two great lights, the great light to rule by day and the small light to rule by night." Initially, theSunand the Moon are established as luminaries which possess equal greatness whereas the next part of the line describes a very definite difference in status: theSunis called great whereas the Moon is described as small. According to the Talmud, this very specific wording alludes to the fact that initially the Sun and the Moon were of equal stature but then a regression occurred. The light of the Moon was dimmed so that she became a reflector of the Sun's light instead of being a generator of light. The sun, though, retained its radiance (Schneider, 2001).

In fact, the Moon's regression is alluded to in prayers which Jews recite when sanctifying the Moon every month. The prayer book includes the following prayer:

> "May it be your will, G-d . . . to fill the flaw of the Moon that there be no more a diminution in it. May the light of the Moon be like the light of theSunand like the light of the seven days of creation, as it was before it diminished, as it said: "And G-d made two great lights . . . (as quoted in Schneider, 2001)."

Quoting the work of Rabbi Isaac Luria, Schneider explains that the Moon and the Sun are direct representatives of the feminine polarity and the masculine polarity. Each of these polarities have many associated symbols and physical representations. According to Rabbi Luria, when the Moon was diminished, the feminine in all its forms and expressions was exiled. Since the whole of the woman's being is associated with the Moon, women was dramatically affected by the Moon's diminishment. Man was also affected since part of his constitution is feminine.

Schneider describes the many implications and consequences that occurred in the aftermath of the Moon's diminishment. She writes,

> No corner of the universe escaped unscathed. Since the world's holographic every piece contains its share of Moon dust. Consequently, no sliver of the universe can achieve perfection until the Moon recoups her losses and recovers her light. As long as the feminine presence within each creature remains diminished, the entire organism lacks completion. Thus, the primal drive of the universe is to restore woman (and all her shattered pieces) back to

her place on high. There is no other way to fix the world except by inviting her back up and in (p. 69).

Now it should be clearer. The feminine dimension of the world shattered. This affected women, very specifically. It also affected the part of each person that is feminine, the unconscious mind. Each self is effectively shattered. Everybody, then, has borne the brunt of the Moon's diminishment. We are all broken, coping with inborn deficits of all kinds, including devastating health problems and the psychological wounds incurred in childhood. We are enduring the litany of losses associated with aging. The women's movement, then, has been divinely decreed, an effort to restore the feminine back to its original stature. The movement to rescue Planet Earth and restore its integrity, same thing. The self-help movement and the evolution of the psychotherapy profession, also divinely decreed, helping people restore the broken feminine aspects of self back to wholeness.

"Help, I've Fallen and I Can't Stand Up"

This is our destiny, to participate in this process of elevating and restoring the Moon to its former state of perfection. Indeed, the culture participates. In 1987, there was a television commercial that basically went viral. It showed a little old lady who had fallen and, using a life call system, pushed the button and spoke to the operator saying, "Help! I've fallen and I can't get up!"

This B grade commercial was actually quite forgettable. Low-budget, running on cable stations and during daytime television for the next few years. This little Mrs. Fletcher, the little old lady in the commercial, became an icon in popular culture! Her line was parodied in countless television shows and movies, included in several songs that became popular. Young people were wearing T-shirts: "Help! I've fallen and I can't get up." Why all the fuss?

I'm going to suggest that any number of marketing campaigns succeed because they are rattling chains that take us back to archetypal truths. In this case, what is the truth? That the feminine has taken a fall and must be raised back to its full stature. These themes have unspoken meaning for consumers. The associations are powerful enough to generate interest in a particular ad campaign or even to inspire consumer loyalty to a given product. Many of these concepts derive from Kabbalah and express the Kabbalah's understanding of the structure of the world while also revealing a mysterious symbolism that pervades daily life, which can help us understand everything from marketing successes to graphic design principles or rules of the road. Much of this material I have covered in an earlier publication, *Reading the Soul: Kabbalah and the Psychology of Handwriting*. Here, I want to suggest that the TV commercial mentioned above went viral because, on an unconscious level, we well know that the feminine has taken a fall and we must help her get back up.

Indeed, these same themes come through in nursery rhymes. Imagine singing "Rock-A-Bye Baby" to a baby. We are singing about a cradle rocking, falling and the baby crashes down, no doubt to get a head injury! What about Humpty Dumpty? Falling off that wall and nobody can fix them and he breaks into a thousand pieces. Kabbalah tells us that we know that the feminine has been diminished and whether we represent it as a baby or an egg, one way or other we are all going to confront the brokenness in this world and we have to do our best to register it, accept it and to try and repair it. It's a process. It's what we are supposed to be working on.

The Ascension of the Feminine

So this is the context for considering the women's movement. But it's not just the emancipation of women; it's also a growing interest in the woman's way. More and more, we are exploring the feminine way as a modus operandi for virtually every endeavor. What is a woman's vision of leadership and how does that differ from that of men? Executives are routinely being trained in emotional intelligence in order to cultivate a more relationship-oriented style of management, representing this feminine style of leadership.

Trend forecaster Faith popcorn and her co-author Lys Marigold (1996) described "FemaleThink" as one of the prominent trends that would continue to revolutionize our lives. They wrote:

> "We've gone through the Year of the Woman, The Decade of the Woman, but we believe we are approaching the Millennium of the Woman. We think that the next thousand years will be the time when women find their true strength and use it for real-world good. A Singapore born woman trader on Wall Street, Mei Ping Yang, a wizard with numbers, pointed out an interesting theory: all the dates in this past thousand years started off with the number one, a MaleThink number, independent, direct, ego-concentrated, singular. But . . . Starting with the year 2000 and going on the next thousand years will be leading off with the number 2. And "2' is definitely a more basically female number. Two: partnerships, familial teamwork, a balance of power, being relational, FemaleThink."

In this context, we can track the progress of the feminine. Calling out sexual abuse in the "Me, too" movement, women finding their place in the workforce, any number of ways women have achieved breakthroughs in a wide range of fields. The task at hand is to elevate the feminine. Ever wonder why a groom carries his bride over the threshold? He is elevating her and, hopefully, setting an intention to elevate (and not to topple) the feminine over the course of that marriage. She will express her experience of elevation in different ways, one of which was an "imponderable" for David Feldman (1993). Feldman has authored a series of books which attempts to explain curious facts about the world we live in. Let's look at why women sometimes kick their legs up when kissing their boyfriends or husbands in public.

Feldman tried to come up with an explanation for this puzzling gesture that we have seen in movies or, perhaps, experienced. In an effort to understand and explain the gesture, he came up with some fairly weak hypotheses and then invited his readers to come up with better theories. In accordance with the ideas presented here, I would argue that a woman is so elevated by a happy partnership with a man that she expresses this elevation symbolically in a moment of contact with her significant other. According to Jewish mystical thought, the most feminine part of the body is the foot. She elevates her foot, an expression of the elevation she is experiencing. In Jewish writings a man is directed to elevate his wife by making him the crown he wears on his head. There it is. The elevation.

Other reversals which serve to elevate the feminine: When a couple get married, he wears black, the color associated with *Yin*. She wears white, the color associated with *Yang*. She puts forward her finger (associated with the line, the archetype of masculinity) and he brings a ring (the circle is the archetype of the feminine) for her. He commits his feminine, the circle, and she offers her masculine, the finger, to consecrate that commitment. There's the reversal again! And when she wears the color associated with Yang, she moves into a the power position of *Yang*. She is emboldened. She is elevated.

How Mary Helped

Now we come back to the Mary Tyler Moore Show. Launched in the 70s, as the women's movement was really heating up, the culture is faced with a challenge. The feminine must be raised. How should this be done? Now, in the 2020s, we see young women wearing hats designed to replicate female anatomy. We see young women slamming their fists on the door of the Supreme Court.

We see feminist marches devolving into a platform for virulent anti-Semitism. The feminist movement has taken a decidedly untoward turn.

Many of us who identified as feminists in the 70s and 80s distance ourselves from the current feminist movement. Mary, though, was a role model, showing women of her generation how they could take strides forward without categorically rejecting the contributions of the 'white men' – the Mr. Grant's – who had, for example, set up working electricity grids and built hospitals. She was hesitant, sometimes stammering, sometimes unsure how to put that foot forward, other times finding the power and confidence to thrust. She showed us how we could do *Yang* but maintain femininity.

I didn't appreciate Mary Richards as a role model back when I was 15. Now when I see what the feminist movement has devolved into, I treasure the vision she planted: independence, the importance of the BFF, complexities navigating the power hierarchy, doing all the above with delicacy. Never slamming anyone. Never collapsing into extremism or one-sided polemics. How very Jewish! To take on the task, working laboriously to elevate the fallen Moon, but to be a *mensch*, a good egg, while doing it.

And Mary was a *mensch*. She refused to smoke on-screen. In real life, she smoked three packs a day. She did not want to be the cause of any young woman succumbing to this terrible addiction, influenced by her. Based on what I observe in today's feminist movement, I come to the conclusion that a whole generation of women might have been more more resentful and more unhealthy if we hadn't have had a Mary Tyler Moore/Mary Richards showcasing one way to climb the ladder of success and otherwise help the Moon back up on her (metaphoric) feet.

And, to add to her merit, where Lucille Ball got her laughs by doing a job poorly, Mary Richards was the keener who always strived to be impeccable, moral, conscientious. That impulse was the genesis of her humor, not a conniving effort to defy authority figures. How often do we see the opposite profile, the rebel, as protagonist in TV shows or movies? Often!

I conjecture the wholesome character she depicted brought a new face to comedy. She wasn't mean, sarcastic, catty. Her comedy was self-effacing. In a culture where much humor is negative, Mary's brand was nobler, kinder. And, I believe for this, she, her production, her troupe, were blessed.

The Prideful, Angry Sun

Back to Genesis. In the Talmud, some commentators assert that it was the Sun, itself, that argues that the Moon should be diminished. Schneider describes the Sun as the ego that does not like to see its flaws reflected back by the Moon. In the Talmud's narrative, the Sun barks at the Moon, "Diminish yourself! Make yourself small!"

I think part of the gift of the MTM Show was to role model how we need to relate to unrectified Sun types. Think of Lou Grant, the cranky director of the news on the MTM Show. He interviews Mary for the Assistant Producer job. He looks at her and says emphatically, "You've got spunk!" She says, "Thank you." He says: "I HATE spunk." Typical unrectified Sun!!

Another unrectified Sun: Newscaster Ted Baxter. So egoic. So narcissistic. Regardless of the unrectified Suns in her midst, Mary pays homage, calling Lou, "Mr. Grant." She is a feminist but she does not begrudge the hierarchy. She casts her sights upward but doesn't perceive the white man ,at the top of the hierarchy, as her enemy. She accommodates or even submits to his errant ways. Mary Tyler Moore, herself, will get to great heights, launching a production company, producing very successful sitcoms, all motored by a mentality that she, personally, shares with the characters she played. She has, by the way, stated time and time again that Mary Richards and Laura Petrie, both, were characters much like her own personality style and nature.

The ascension of the Moon. How many female writers did she employ, giving young comediennes a voice in an industry which was otherwise dominated by men? How much success did she achieve, despite a difficult family history and her own bout of alcoholism? She showed us that poise, gratitude, deference and grace are tools in our toolkit. How far we get if we use them in our quest to address power imbalances and help the Moon achieve its promised ascension.

Mary as Moon

Notice the symbolism. Rhoda called Mary, "Mare." Mare, a female work horse! Of course, spelled differently, we have the French word, mere, which means mother. And what about Mary Richards' colleague, Murray Slater and his wife Marie. Mary, Murray, Marie. The light of the Moon, the feminine, background players representing the light of the Moon which shines quietly at night. People who participate in an endeavor and are behind the scenes. They are not the leaders, at the top of the hierarchy. That would be Lou. They are not the public figures, the talking heads, the ones who get the attention. That would be Ted.

Mary: the concept of marrying theSunand the Moon. How do we bring together the different forms of unrectified masculinity (pride and aggression, Ted and Lou) and create a working system. Mary would mediate that. Other people, like Sue Ann Nivins, showing the human polarities: her sweetness and helpfulness versus her cattiness and lust. Phyllis, another character to shine the light of narcissism and egocentricity. Valerie Harper, who played Rhoda, used to say that in those three characters, Mary,

Rhoda and Phyllis, Mary was who you wanted to be, Phyllis is who you hoped you were not and imperfect 'rough around the edges' Rhoda is "who you probably are."

Paradox and Maturity

Bear in mind that according to Kabbalah, spiritual maturity manifests in the ability to host paradox. These days, it's too easy to fall into extremes. Marital research echoes the importance of the qualities we are talking about here, to bring feminine grace to the cause of assertiveness, otherwise associated with *Yang*.

John Gottman is a world leader in the area of marital research. He can watch a tape of a couple who are married talking about their areas of conflict and he can know with 97% accuracy which of these couples will still be married in five years. What's remarkable about this feat is that he gets this accuracy rating by watching only a short snippet of the tape of them speaking – without the volume playing! He's not listening to the words!

In a couple who are destined to divorce, Gottman sees extreme disdain and disgust evident in one or both partners. If he is seeing negativity without redeeming gestures, warmth or positivity, a smile, a touch, a kind gesture, he is looking at impending divorce. When he sees a couple arguing, but *intermittently* joking, smiling, otherwise diffusing the tension, this is a marriage that will last. *Yang* (anger, intensity) needs *Yin* (gestures of affiliation) or the marriage falls into states characterized by extreme aggression and resentment. A partner deploys *Yin* to remind the other of affection, camaraderie, to otherwise express a team mentality.

Of course, the same holds true in the political landscape. Falling to extremes has people aligning with dangerous ideologies and demonizing those on the other side. Dialogue becomes impossible. In this climate, we need Mary! As mentioned earlier, Mary is on record of saying that the character that was depicted in the show really was her, her personality. These are Mary's words, describing herself:

> "I'm cautious in my dealings. I'm a hang back person. When things get uncomfortable, I'm reserved, I guess. I'm precise. I'm never late to anything, always ahead of time and waiting. I tend to be moderate. Some people think I'm very conservative and sometimes I am."

Boy, could we use that archetype and influence in this day and age.

The Three Amigos

Let's revisit the 3 archetypes of Mary, Rhoda and Phyllis. In Kabbalah[1], there are three categories of people: the righteous one, the *tzadik*, the evil one, the *rasha*, and what is called in Hebrew, the *benoni*, the in-between. Mary, with her perfect manners, embodies the righteous one, she who Sue Ann Nivins finds disgustingly chaste.

Mary was specifically role modelling the *Yin* of *Yang*. Her character was aspiring for professional accomplishment (*Yang*) but she brought a gentleness to the task (*Yin*). We are saying that the perfected way to do anything is in a centrist way where we have some *Yin*, some *Yang*, at play. When we architect ourselves, modulating both masculine and feminine aspects, softening extremes in the personality, we are channeling the Hebrew letter *Hey*.

Then there is Rhoda, rough around the edges but she really wants to be good. She is our *benoni*', the one 'in between.' Phyllis, in the grips of self-deception and self-interest is the *rasha*. Unknown to Mary and Rhoda, Phyllis and her husband were the property managers of that house where they all lived. When anything broke, they never returned the phone calls for repair! When Mary casually told Phyllis about a plumbing problem, Phyllis

---

1. My source here is the Tanya.

encouraged her to just get it fixed herself and pay someone privately because the property owner was slow to deal with these matters!

The Mary Tyler Moore Show was a morality play. We could laugh as we would watch the various characters negotiate situations. They captured the three positions, the human landscape, and perhaps, with the aid of laughter, could help us negotiate our own and others foibles with a bit more levity.

This is the legacy that she has left. She showed us: when navigating significant reversals, when redressing power imbalances that go back to the beginning of time, care should be taken to do it with delicacy and caution. The insignia she came up with for her production company MTM was a little kitten making a meow, standing in contrast to another production company, Metro-Goldwyn-Mayer which had a lion in its insignia, issuing a loud roar. There's an expression, "tread softly and carry a big stick." You can't argue her success and accomplishment. She definitely had a big stick. But she also tread softly. Women in her generation learned from her greatness. Today's generation can learn from . . . Lady Gaga? Who is our current generation's ambassador of Grace? Nikki Haley, I guess. How many magnificent role models are there? Find people whose language patterns you would wish to emulate. That's the criteria I would use.

> I live in a type of controlled awareness. I wouldn't call it fear, but it's an awareness. I know I have an obligation to behave in a certain way. And I am able to do that.'"

Mary Tyler Moore

Stage 2 of the CBS Studio Centre has been adorned with a plaque which reads: "On this stage a company of talented and loving friends produced a television classic: The Mary Tyler Moore

Show 1970-1977." Indeed. If you're in Connecticut and you happen to the Oak Lawn Cemetery where she rests, make sure you bring a stone to leave on her monument. And, please, . . . a favor. Put one there for me.

5.

Why the Poor Schlemiel?

Comedy writer Steve Kaplan describes comedy in the following way: "it's about an ordinary person struggling against insurmountable odds without many of the required skills and tools with which to win, yet never giving up hope." Kaplan is right. Any number of times the character who we watch in comedies is the *schlemiel*, a Yiddish word which implies the poor loser who struggles.

In the Mary Tyler Moore Show, Rhoda was the classic example. Struggling with weight problems, social rejection and bad luck, certain plot lines could only happen to Rhoda. In one show, she is excited to introduce Mary to her new suitor, the fellow she is sure she's going to marry. Of course, he meets Mary and is immediately taken with her and dumps Rhoda. Poor Rhoda!

What about the time, in the subsequent Rhoda series: Rhoda has the bad fortune of losing control of a costume rack on a busy New York main street. The rack swerves into the path of a cop riding his horse. The horse jumps lanes and gets hit by a car. Rhoda has inadvertently killed a horse! Rhoda goes to make a sales call for window design services, breaks reams of china in the shop, then has a heated meeting with the business owner who had thought he was going to have a dalliance/sales call from Myrna, Rhoda's assistant. Only Rhoda could have such bad luck!

Rhoda, herself, was well aware of her destiny, the subject of many of her quips. About the proceedings of a given day, Rhoda says to Mary:

> "You're having a lousy streak. I happen to be having a terrific streak. Soon the world will be back to normal. Tomorrow you will meet a crown head of Europe and marry. I will have a fat attack, eat 3,000 peanut butter cups, and die."

Indeed, the negativity in her life will constantly be the topic of her one-liners; she, the brunt of her own jokes. After she gets married, she tells Joe: "Remember when we got married – all those nasty rumors that our relationship would never last? (Pause). I must admit, I was wrong."

Mary needs to borrow a dress. Rhoda presents some options. Rhoda: "That looks completely different off the hanger . . . Worse."

Why the *Schlemiel*?

Why do we need the *schlemiel* in our comedies? Rhoda normalizes the fact that life makes us all *schlemiels*. Life is hard. When she is struggling to find an apartment in New York City, she reflects, "I remember a time we used to read obituaries to find an apartment. Now, someone coughs, you follow them around!"

Brenda finally announces to Rhoda that she is dating someone. Delighted, Rhoda says to her sister, another *schlemiel*: "And you are the one who kept saying, 'I'll never meet anyone, it will never happen, I'll spend my entire life drifting aimlessly from one Baskin-Robbins to another'." Later, it becomes clear that the guy

Brenda is dating is actually married. Rhoda: "Why can't the Girl Scouts print a manual for adults? They teach you to spot poison oak and then let you walk right through a patch of married men." Ah, the plight of *schlemiels*.

Life is not easy. The reality is that, relative to our discussion of the last chapter, we are all meant to live the plight of the Moon. We are all diminished. We have all been rejected. We all struggle against life. Not everybody gets to be Mary, beautiful, good, well-dressed, well loved. More than likely, we are the imperfect Moon that needs to be rectified. We are Rhoda. We wear our foibles. We say the wrong thing at the wrong time. We 'get' Rhoda, unlucky in love. Our affection for Rhoda can help us find affection for our own bumbling ways, the inner Rhoda, the *schlemiel* in all of us.

The Alchemist

But is Rhoda a loser? Rhoda is actually an alchemist. The alchemist that each one of us needs to become. Why?

Rhoda mutates the negativity that life serves up and turns it into fodder for jokes. Rhoda role models thousands of years of Jewish survival, coping by being funny, inspiring others to take it in the chin and have a good attitude, in so doing, prevailing. Who gets the last laugh?

If negative circumstances provide the inspiration to reach into the realm where everything connects with everything else, the realm of transcendence, if it becomes the stimulus for a wickedly funny line, then maybe the whole thing was worth it! She moves from loser to victor. Another reversal! She will be the spokesperson of the indomitable Jewish spirit. The Jews are meant to be a light unto the nations! No wonder there are so many Jewish comedians! With Jewish names lit up in the marquees around the nation, Jews are teaching people how to rise above troubles with a shot of humor.

Coming up with a eulogy for the oldest living citizen of Minneapolis, Rhoda writes: "Wee Willie Williams was the oldest living citizen of Minneapolis. There were other citizens of Minneapolis who were older . . . but they happen to be dead."

Finding Strength in Weakness (not 'Wokeness')

Could we walk in Rhoda's footsteps and perform this sort of alchemy, turning straw into gold, mutating negative circumstances into the laughter of transcendence? It's something we should try to do. When we mentioned Chinese philosophy, we noted that *Laozi* urges us away from being willful and imposing our vision on circumstances. Wielding power goes against the Way. Writes Puett and Gross-Loh (2016), "the enduring power of the *Laozi* lies in its potential to help one become infinitely more influential through softness, not hardness; through connecting, not dominating (p. 146)."

In other words, we have to move to a very different frame, understanding that there is strength to be had in weakness. This is not a teaching that intrinsically attracts followers in the Western world. But if we look carefully, as do the authors just mentioned, we find examples of people who lead using the strategy of the Moon, not the sun.

Puett and Gross-Loh cite Rosa Parks as one example. A mild-mannered black woman, Rosa Parks refused to give up her seat on the bus to a white passenger, possessing a clear knowing that a quiet response would be her best way of proceeding. Right out of the Mary Tyler Moore playbook!

The authors cite the way Ronald Reagan won his presidential elections. It's ironic that one of the concerns in his second presidential run was whether Reagan, at his age, would be at risk of dementia during his span as president. Indeed, he did succumb to dementia while in office. Yet, his mastery at the presidential debate sealed the election for him. Standing next to the opposing candidate, many years younger, Reagan was asked if he, himself might be too old to serve again as President of the United States. Reagan responded, " I am not going to exploit, for political purposes, my opponent's youth and inexperience." Big laugh! No defensiveness. No pride. A kindly response in good humor. Touché! Reagan was back for a second term!

Laozi wrote, "The Way constantly does nothing, yet nothing is not done." In the Tao Cheng, written in the 11th century, we read:

> Of all the elements, the Sage should take water as his preceptor. Water is yielding but all-conquering. . . . finding itself likely to be defeated, [it] escapes as steam and re-forms. Water washes away Soft Earth, or, when confronted by rocks, seeks a way around. Water corrodes Iron, etc."

Yin, a fertile posture, a gentle manner that can help us win when we otherwise might lose. We need incentives to get us to assume that kindly, low-status demeanor. The *schlemiel* is our ticket. Or *schlemiel*, en route to the most creative role of all: trickster, the identity of the healthy comedian, the one who uses humor for good, and so role models the task of alchemy for all of us.

6.

Mary & Rhoda, Rachel & Leah: Learning from Biblical Archetypes

In this chapter, we detour, to reflect on the way the Mary Tyler Moore Show focused our attention on the BFF friendship and put that friendship on the map. Beautiful Mary, jealous Rhoda; conventional Mary, quirky Rhoda; beloved Mary, rejected Rhoda. In fact, you find a similar pairing in the more contemporary sitcom, Grace and Frankie.

Ever wonder whether there are classic archetypes at play when we watch a beautiful protagonist and her artistic, less polished, out-of-the-box sidekick? I would tell you 'yes'. Turns out we can learn a lot about ourselves and our friends if we better unpack these prototypes. Who are they? And, further, who are they within us? Jewish wisdom provides interesting insights.

Rabbi YY Jacobson notes that each Torah personality we read about represents an individual that lived but also a timeless characteristic that exists within every human personality. In the case of two sisters who are destined to become wives of the patriarch, Jacob, these two represent two very different distinct aspects of the human psyche.

Rachel & Leah: Conscious and Unconscious

Leah, the elder sister, corresponds to the unconscious and deeply internal aspects of self, those aspects that necessarily defy expression in words. Jacob was tricked into marrying Leah. She was the rejected wife, deeply sensitive and perceptive, she suffered the ills of the world more acutely, was more subject to tears.

The Torah describes her as having weak or dim eyes. Commentators note that she looked with deep intensity. She had that look of deep apperception, she saw to the core of situations and people. As a result, Leah suffered more, she took things to heart.

Rachel, in contrast, was the woman Jacob wanted to marry. The name Rachel derives from the Hebrew word that corresponds to Ewe, a female sheep. Rachel was docile, peaceful, unperturbed. She was beautiful but not complicated. Rachel's gift was expression and mastery of the practical, predictable world. Socially gifted, a character that we easily understand, she is the master of pleasantries and fits in any environment, qualifies for any job, effortlessly masters the tasks the world would have her do. Rachel, we get.

The complicated, brooding Leah, always thinking, always analyzing, lives in a higher dimension. Constantly processing abstractions and values, she doesn't fit into our everyday paradigm. Society is more apt to reject Leah. And to celebrate Rachel.

In the Jewish vernacular, Rachel represents speech and Leah represents thought. Rachel is the master of the 'Revealed world', the social and concrete world, the stuff of everyday life. Leah is in touch with the 'Hidden world', a higher world. She is unconventional, the artist, the musician, the muse. And Leah only finds a home in the revealed world when she partners with Rachel. Hence the prototypical BFF partnership!

It's no coincidence that the Mary Tyler Moore Show centered around a pretty, personable, pleasant Mary Richards. It's no coincidence that Mary produced the news. The Mary in each of us is the speaker, the one who can explain, the one with the basic comprehension of that which is everyday and matter-of-fact. That show presented the Rachel prototype and introduced us to Leah.

Rhoda: brilliantly witty, rough around the edges, blurting out that which most would never think to say, coming up with ingenious insights and subject to constant rejection ("Hello. I'm the other person in the room.").

Long-suffering, Rhoda has a difficult time in the revealed world. Everything goes wrong! She doesn't find an easy home here! Or as Rhoda puts it, on the one day when Mary is in a funk and Rhoda is doing well:

> You're having a lousy streak. I happen to be having a terrific streak. Soon the world will be back to normal. Tomorrow you will meet a crown head of Europe and marry. I will have a fat attack, eat 3,000 peanut butter cups, and die.

When Rhoda graduates to her own show, she becomes the Rachel character and her sister, Brenda, is the new Leah, self-deprecating, consistently rejected.

On the other hand, our Leah character is always unabashedly herself. She doesn't succumb to social pressure. Leah represents the zone of internality. Such characters never lose the pulse of their own unique originality.

In contrast, the sages teach, the Rachel character can fall into exile, lose her voice, succumb to social pressure. In the Torah, Rachel represents the *Shechina*, the aspect of Divinity that has been exiled from this world. So the Rachel's of this world have their own problems. Too often, they lose their voice and stray from their truth, often in the context of relationship. They partly find themselves, though, in their pairing with Leah.

And so you have the prototypes: the zany creative and the beautiful ingénue. Each the master of their own domain. The two archetypes work marvelously as a team.

Look around. You'll often see this BFF pairing in the world at large. With every successful partnership, the two domains of the world, the hidden and the revealed, are better bridged. The Mary/ Grace character is the master of competence and social convention. The Rhoda/Frankie character brings flavor, insight and novelty into the moment. Rachel is order. Leah has her finger on the pulse of that which is unknown, ephemeral or otherworldly. Leah is 'out there', but her perspective is fresh, interesting and important.

The Rachel and Leah Within

Life is full of complexities; for the Rachel's and Leah's in the world; also for the ones we each find, within. The inner Rachel has mastered social mores but sometimes fails to access her own inner truth. The inner Leah houses your idiosyncrasies and aspects of self that are inaccessible, sometimes only channeled through art, poetry or via dreams at night. Rachel is your Sun. Leah is your Moon.

Our first reaction to Leah, whether the one within or the one in the world at large, is rejection. Rabbi Jacobson points out that we hate that which we don't understand. When someone or something is too deep, too incomprehensible, our first response is to deny it or delegitimize it. The inner Leah hosts aspects of the world that are unintelligible, confusing, even overwhelming.

And yet, we must divine down more complex aspects of reality . . . and ourselves. If we will sit with the Leah dimension, reject the urge to turn away, we will befriend imminent aspects of reality (and self) that will expand our lives and our paradigms. We will be better for it.

In fact, the more you integrate your own Leah, the more you can partner with the Leah dimension of your spouse. As Jordan Peterson would say, we have to master the domain of the familiar, but also extend a tendril into the unknown. We have to open to aspects of self and world that don't make sense. We have to figure them out. And escort them in to our lives.

You only really get to marry Rachel – and have a life characterized by acceptance – when you marry Leah – first. And so you watch Mary and Rhoda or Frankie and Grace to get a whiff how one might achieve such an inter-inclusion. Watching the social dance between these two archetypes helps us architect and bring together the two prototypes we harbor within.

Long live our BFF's, connecting us to a landscape that is variable and complex, showing us how the other half lives and bringing us into deeper resonance . . . with ourselves![1]

1. Reprinted with permission from the Times of Israel blog.

7.

Bungee Jumping on
Planet Earth

Gary, making overtures to Rhoda: "Have you ever slept in a waterbed?"

Rhoda, glaring, angry: "Have you ever slept in a hospital bed?"

This is a book about reversals. Time and time again, we are going to have to make some pretty dramatic 'about faces' in our lives. There's something to be said for being a person who can tell a joke or a funny story; or being somebody who can tolerate a dramatic change in life circumstances, negative, not just positive, and adapt appropriately. There's something to be said for being a person who hosts Divinity in such a way that he or she merits Divine cooperation so that, against all odds, negative circumstances mutate, becoming (unexpectedly) positive. There is something to be said for being a person who can "turn a nothing day and suddenly make it all seem worthwhile."

This is my next claim. If we will let go of egoic, prideful and will-based behavior, if we will reverse into a more receptive, nuanced, feminine position, we will sometimes be the beneficiaries of amazing reversals, of the sort that we, ourselves, could never manage to architect. And we may, ultimately, become the type who can channel alchemy!

What does all this look like?

Think of something that happened to the devoutly religious Marie Osmond. She had planned a trip to speak to a young women's leadership conference and was bringing one of her teenagers along. As she was packing up, Marie was plagued with the notion that she would bring her baby along. Her youngest was 3 years old, not toilet trained yet. Imagine managing a toddler while negotiating travel *and* speaking obligations! The idea was madness. Yet, it kept popping to mind. Finally, she grabbed diapers. The baby was coming, too.

That night, Marie received a call. One of her kids lit a broom on fire and then mindlessly put the broom in the garage. Hours later, some fuel in the garage exploded. Two rooms of the house – above the garage – were destroyed: Marie's office and the bedroom of the two daughters who were now safely by her side. All this happened in the middle of the night! Without doubt, her baby would have perished in that explosion.

It's good to have friends in high places! These wonderful favors can sometimes be accessed by those who make it their business to be a vessel for the light of Divinity.

Humor gives us a whiff of what is possible. We get that pleasant euphoric feeling. That's fun. But what it is really trying to do is to get us to take on reversal as a way of life. You need to know what reversal can do for you. You need to make friends with it. Of course, we all like 'rags to riches' stories, but sometimes there are 'riches to rags' stories and we also have to navigate those reversals en route to getting somewhere new. Now I want to tell you a few stories.

Big Joe

For many years I've been inspired by the work of Dr. Milton Erickson, a psychiatrist who, himself, experienced a lifetime of crippling health problems. He never felt self-pity. In fact, he felt that poor health was his best education. He felt it was his advantage, something that helped him achieve success in his clinical role.

Growing up, Erickson lived in a rural locale. It was a small town and when he was a boy there was a teenager, Big Joe, who had achieved a degree of infamy. Big Joe was a delinquent. He would spend six months in jail, be released, and it was only a matter of time until he was thrown back into jail. Things would go missing. Eventually, somebody would catch him in the act and back to the slammer, he would go.

In this story, true story, Big Joe has been released from jail. Stuff is missing. It just takes a little bit of time until they have just cause to throw him back in jail. One day, he is walking through a clearing, a path in the forest and walking in the opposite direction, coming towards him, is a beautiful tall young woman. Struck by what he sees, this 6′ 5″ fellow blocks her passage. She stands there. He's glaring at her. He barks out, "Will you go with me to the dance Friday night?" She glares at him and barks back: "If you're a gentleman, I will." He steps away allowing her passage. She marches on. Over the next few days, property that had been stolen reappears, left for the rightful owners, in the cover of night.

Friday night. They both show up at the dance. They spend the night dancing.

Fast-forward: he becomes a farmhand on her father's farm. He works there and eventually he marries her. He moves from the domain for farmhands to the family dwelling and when her parents die, he and she both manage the farm. They never had children. What they did do, though: they went to the jail to find out who was on parole, each time they needed to hire a farmhand. They hired these boys. Some of them disappeared in the middle of the night, never to be seen or, eventually finding their way back to jail. Others, rehabilitated themselves, made good. He had resolved to help other boys to turn themselves around. When the couple died, they left that land to the local society whose agenda was to help rehabilitate young men. Nice reversal, no?

Milton Erickson used to say that sometimes psychotherapy is short: six words long: "if you're a gentleman, I will." That's all it took.

The first story is an example of how an encounter with somebody, a chance event, can be a turning point, all that we need to tip ourselves into a reversal that is overdue, something we've been needing to change about ourselves. My second story is an example how sometimes we can motor this reversal without a particular trigger in the environment. Sometimes something awakens from deep within.

Leaving a Lifestyle Behind

Dr. Rabbi Abraham Twerski is a prominent psychiatrist who has been very influential in the field of addictions. He tells a story about a client he met when he was doing his psychiatric residency in a hospital, so many years ago. Here is the story that he told:

A woman, let's call her Karen, was the daughter of a minister and rebelled against her parents values. She got very involved in drinking but ultimately married and had two children. Her alcoholism was a problem for her family. Her husband gave her an ultimatum. "It's either the alcohol or us." She chose the alcohol. She left the marriage.

Left with the need to support herself, she took up a rather unsavory vocation. She persisted with her abuse of alcohol and over time was hospitalized 100 times for medical problems related to her alcoholism. One day, she spontaneously sought consultation of a lawyer and had him draw up paperwork that would commit her to an institution for one full year. She would not be able to leave the institution. She was seeking treatment for herself.

At the end of that year, she was no longer drinking. She was released and took a job as a nanny for a lawyer. He was alcoholic. She tried to manage him and keep him functional so he could continue with his career despite his alcoholism. She wanted to try and reclaim a relationship with her children. She contacted her husband. He said to her, "I told them you died." So she lived quietly, working at a respectable job, and sought psychotherapy with Dr. Twerski at the local hospital.

The psychiatrist was amazed. She continued to grow, cultivate insight, find some meaning in her life, up until her death a number of years later.

Hillman reflects,

> "We all have to chew and swallow the errors and misfortunes, sprinkled well with the salt of remorse, of what had previously been two-dimensional memoranda, flat like pages from a calendar, simply things that happened without pattern, without meaning. Life review yields long-term gains that enrich character by bringing understanding to events. The patterns in your life become more discernible among the wreckage and the romance, more like a well-plotted novel that reveals characters through their actions and reactions. Life review is really nothing other than rewriting — or writing for the first time — the story of your life, or writing your life into stories. And without stories there is no pattern, no understanding, no art, and no character — merely habits, events

passing before the eyes of an aimless observer, a life unreviewed, a life lost in the living of it (p. 132)."

And this she did. She processed her life. He met her for weekly sessions for quite a few years. That psychiatrist always wondered, though, how was it that she managed to break her pattern of self-destruction, found the strength and resolve to secure the services of a lawyer and thereby to access a better life for herself. From our vantage point, we can say that there is this capacity to access the reversal at virtually any minute, against all odds. There is a reservoir within that we can call on. We must know this.

The Thumb-Sucker

Another story. Because sometimes a therapist is the person who will help us animate the reversal. My favorite therapist is the late psychiatrist Milton Erickson, of course. So you get a story from his magical collection. To read more creative examples of the most magnificent therapeutics, you can pick up Jay Haley's *Uncommon Therapy: The Psychiatric Techniques of Dr. Milton H Erickson*. In this story, a family have come in to seek treatment for little Johnny who continues sucking his thumb well past the age. The parents have become so agitated with his regressive habit that they call him out constantly and the house has devolved into power struggles and screaming.

Erickson calls in the parents. Once he understands the scope of the problem, he tells the parents in no uncertain terms, "Johnny is my client. You are not to talk to Johnny about thumb sucking. He is my client. Only I will talk to Johnny about what he does with his thumb." Erickson orders the parents out of the room. They have been dethroned. Now *schlemiels*, they slink out of the room. Johnny is empowered.

Erickson says to Johnny, "Now Johnny, a little five-year-old has every right to suck his thumb and, not only that, there are tremendous benefits to thumb sucking. For example, when you suck your thumb, you create wonderful stimulation to that digit. The blood flows and it's very healthy to help that thumb get big and strong. But," Erickson added, "you fail to realize that you have nine other digits, eight fingers and one other thumb, and they all need the circulation, as well."

Erickson now gave him some homework: "every time you suck your thumb, I'm going to require you to taking a turn sucking each finger sequentially and then sucking the other thumb." You certainly can't play favorites in life!

Erickson gave this exercise to the boy, requiring that any time he wanted to suck his thumb he would do the full job. And he added, "by the time you turn six, you will be a big boy, you will not want to suck your thumb anymore. You have to do this exercise now, while you're a little five-year-old." For the next six months, this boy could drive his parents crazy, have the final say and be the master of his fate while he did this tedious task of sucking all his fingers (making him a *schlemiel*, too). Sure enough, when he turned six, he no longer had to maintain this labor. Johnny stopped, of his own accord. Reversal complete.

Reversals Are Delicious!

We've all had reversals in our lives, many for which we are most grateful! I loved the bumper sticker: "I always use words that are soft and sweet just in case I have to eat them!" How many things that we swore we would be doing off into the future we quietly gave up – happily gave up – with the dawning of maturity? How many of our attitudes have changed 180°? Reversals are delicious, the stuff of life, and we need more of them.

One line I say to my psychotherapy clients when we are doing an assessment: "let's figure out what your symptom wants to be when it grows up!" Any symptom really is there in an effort to architect the kind of progress which is the ultimate successful reversal of the symptom! It really doesn't want you to be suffering forever! It's like a labor pain. It's trying to birth into the next thing.

Recommended Reading

How can we be privy to these delicious reversals? One thing I recommend is the right reading. So many times people have these reversals and write amazing books. Read them! Some of my favorites:

The Prizewinner of Ohio: How My Mother Raised 10 Children on 25 Words or Less by Terry Ryan. What a story. This woman, the writer's mother, was married to an alcoholic and she had to figure out how to keep the family afloat, all the while functioning as a stay at home mom. She entered every contest in the 50s where you could win a toaster or a bread maker or small prizes. What a story! A Catholic woman who honored the institution of marriage and not only did she win enough to keep her family afloat but G-d helped! Just when the family was going to lose everything, she won a car! Such an inspiring story! I keep this book on my bookshelf!

Recently I read *The Honey Bus: A Memoir of Loss, Courage and a Girl Saved by Bees* by Meredith May. You must read it! This woman's mother had terrible psychiatric problems and a terrible temper but her grandfather and his aviary saved her. Everything she needed to learn about how to function in an organized harmonious way with others, she learned from bees. This book is a 'Wow'!

Sometimes a work of fiction can walk you through this process. Pick up *The Manticore* by Robertson Davies. This about a man, middle-aged, who undergoes his own reversal process, one that naturally happens at midlife. We call it the midlife crisis, in this case one that presents an opportunity for growth and self insight.

The book chronicles a psychotherapy process. A magnificent book. One that can help stimulate your own evolution.

There are some books where somebody will show you how a particular practice or interest can be a game changer. For that kind of book, I recommend *10% Happier: How I Tamed the Voice in My Head, Reduce Stress without Losing My Edge and found Self-Help That Actually Works* by Dan Harris. Harris, a newscaster, was caught up in cocaine use and an unhealthy lifestyle, often associated with the high life, namely, his work in the media. Through an interesting evolution he became very active first learning meditation and then practicing meditation and, voila! A magnificent reversal! Now he is an active advocate of meditation and leads a healthy lifestyle!

And you thought you would be reading about laughter and humor! Another reversal! Little did you realize that what lays behind laughter and humor is so monumental, so important, that the euphoria of laughter is mere sugarcoating that gets us to show up and take interest in the topic. The ultimate humor is the deep satisfaction of being able to look back on a life and realize how the impossible happened; that your life transmuted away from what it should have become into the opposite, more productive direction, against all odds.

Tell Lady Gaga. "Born this way" is nonsense. Abraham and Sarah get the last laugh on this one. Having a baby in their 90's, they proved even birth itself is subject to curious and shimmering possibilities. Even what seem to be the most hard-edged rules and terms can be reversed, against all odds, and with a little alchemical participation on your part in tandem with the effort of the One Above. Ha!

8.

"Metaphors Be with You"

So here we are. Laughter. It can take us to higher heights. It can inflict terrible torment. I recall a prominent comedienne who did comedy sketches imitating a celebrity with a speech defect. One time this comic attended a Hollywood party. The public figure she routinely impersonated was in attendance. This comedienne excused herself, went to the bathroom, and vomited. Her act was popular, it certainly made her rich. Spiritually, though, it was no good. Not for her. Not for the person who she shamed.

There's another prominent performer who, many years ago, would routinely make jokes about the emaciated state of a popular singer. One day this performer attended a gala and met the singer, who, owing to her own innate graciousness, made no mention of the nasty jokes. The performer was awash with guilt. Later, even more so. This singer died of anorexia.

Disrupting Order

As a society, we are polluted. In Genesis, the whole point of the narrative of the creation process is to show the direction of progress. Initially, there is chaos, followed by an ordering process.

We are told the benefits of that ordering process: "it was good." We are meant to pursue order.

In culture today, there is an attraction towards disorder. Steve Martin, a comic, did stand up and, in the course of his act, would reach for a glass of water, sip it, then spit the water all over the stage to get the laugh. Today's comedy is about disrupting order.

Rabbi Akiva Tatz:

> "One must realize that the thrill of fitting in is a much more mature experience than the thrill of being a loner at any cost: the immature personality will choose to step out of line in order to experience its own uniqueness; the fact that the overall structure is being betrayed and damaged is not relevant to such an undeveloped mind. Immaturity cannot see the beauty in yielding the self in order to actualize the self; in truth, however, that is the only way to genuine selfhood (Tatz, 1995, p. 81)."

There is a magnificent structure at the core of creation, a structure we are meant to emulate. This structure has been the focus of another book I've written, In *Good Standing: Using Jordan Peterson's Insights on the Structure of Self to Sort Yourself Out*, where I articulate the structure embedded in the world and in our lives. What's relevant here is that there is a structure that we are meant to follow. If we do, we will be the beneficiaries. Our neglect of that structure introduces chaos into our lives. And yet, we continue to defy the structure, begrudge the structure, neglect the structure.

Consider the thoughts of psychologist Michael Ventura who describes a trend he calls "patternless consumerism." Ventura writes,

> "Twenty-four-hour bank call-ins and automatic tellers are in themselves insignificant details of contemporary life. But as part of a pattern, it speaks of a people increasingly coaxed to live without pattern. And increasingly demanding to live without pattern in

terms of services while they bemoan the loss of pattern in their morality, their love life, their thought — and are unconscious of this contradiction."

Who's the poster child of this phenomenon, she who lapsed into disorder despite much talent and advantage? Think of the late Carrie Fisher. She penned the most amazing articulations. I love her phrase, "metaphors be with you." Who thinks like that? Brilliant. In her books, she comes up with gems like that every few lines. But the degree of chaos she was living ultimately killed her. She died on a flight home from abroad, suffering a heart attack while high on cocaine. Her fate was eerily reminiscent of a line she wrote in the voice of her (semi-autobiographical) fictional character: "I shot through my 20s like a luminous thread through a dark needle, blazing toward my destination: nowhere" (1987, p. 16). How ironic that magnificently articulate statement so aptly captured her last moments.

Back to laughter. We have turned the other cheek, failing to see negative consequences of destructive jokes or inflammatory speech. It puts us all in a bad place. In this book, our idea is: to reclaim the best of what laughter can be. How to add positive humor into our lives. How to activate and leverage the healthy reversal mechanism, an essential part of the world's structure, there for our own benefit, central to growth and maturation. What can we each do to get back on track?

As a starting point, I'd like to invite you all to work on speech, improving speech, as a means to rectify the root problem that is societally widespread: a tendency to lapse into chaos which plays out in a myriad of ways, including the celebration and practice of destructive humor and impurity of speech. Can you find a movie where there isn't curse words? To start things off, I tell you a personal story.

Magical Speech

Many years ago, after graduating from a doctoral program, I decided that I wanted to learn hypnosis. Not just learn. Acquire fluency. That's a tall order especially because I wasn't willing to pay a colleague $100 an hour for lessons. Since I was effectively looking to improve my verbal fluency, I made a decision: I was going to stop using any language (and I wasn't using it very frequently) which could be deemed 'low'.

At the same time, I put a free ad in my professional publication to find other therapists interested to study and improve hypnosis skills. What happened? I found a therapist who had been doing a lot of hypnosis, extremely talented, but hadn't done much psychotherapy. I had done a lot of psychotherapy but I hadn't done hypnosis.

We made a plan: each week we would have a telephone meeting to practice together. We did this for one year. At that telephone meeting we would use the language patterns of hypnosis, working on a make-believe client. She was a fabulous hypnotherapist and I marinated in her language patterns; they became mine! One year later . . . I was pretty good! People can pay thousands of dollars to acquire specialized clinical skills. We just helped each other.

Do Try This at Home

I want to offer you a guarantee. If you give up the use of untoward language, you, too, will be rewarded in some way, down the line. Cleaning up your speech is central to personal development. I actually made a video in response to COVID 19. Everybody was walking around with a mask on. I saw potential. Now that we are all wearing masks, what if we use this moment to be conscious of what we are saying and what's coming out of us? "Is this what I'm supposed to be talking about? Are these words I am supposed to be giving voice to?" It's a good moment to change patterns. If you use swearwords, stop! If your habit is to gossip, stop!

If you make significant changes in your language patterns, if you up the bar, speaking in a more inspired and responsible way, I guarantee you there will be benefits. Beyond the benefit I accrued, I've seen others achieve the same good results. Example: one 16-year-old was in the habit of swearing, especially swearing at her parents. One day she reflected that she was the person who always had bad luck. If she was going to the bus stop, just as she gets near, the bus pulls away. She felt like she had some sort of negative cloud that she was standing under, metaphorically speaking. She was open to the idea that all that swearing wasn't working for her. She did the experiment! She removed profanity from her speech. She told me that her luck changed! It was a turning point. Life seemed to work better.

"If you want to know who you are, listen to what you say."
The Maharal

At the time of this writing, I just happened to pick up the recently published autobiography of singer/actor Julie Andrews. In her book, she describes a day years earlier when she was vacationing with the man who would soon become her husband and his children. The children were messy, prompting her to propose a game. If they cleaned their rooms and picked up after themselves, they would win a prize. If they failed to do so, there would be a penalty.

They agreed to her terms but insisted she also had to participate in the game, too. She asked what they wanted her to do as her part of the arrangement. Jenny, Blake's daughter, said, "You have to stop swearing so much." And what was the penalty Julie would pay if she failed to uphold the obligation not to swear? Jenny told her she would have to "write me a story."

Andrews reported she was the first to lose the game! She had to pay up! She started thinking about a story that she would write for her soon-to-be step daughter. That story became the first of dozens of children's books that Andrews has penned, either on her own or with her daughter, Emmy! Expect great things to happen if you abandon profanity. To use Carrie Fisher's quote, my chapter title, I'd like to say that when the force is with us, the right metaphors will be with us, too. Our words will become almost magical. All we need to do is let go of the speech patterns that we would do well to leave behind, anyway!

Let's think about why this might be the case.

How Come?

When you purify yourself, you access more Divinity, you are a clean vessel which can receive what we described as the Hebrew letter *Hey* as it brings its bounty in from above. You get funnier. You pop more easily into that ephemeral space where we make interesting connections. The more negativity within, the more we block the light of Divinity from coming down and enlightening us.

Want more positive reversals? Host more purity. I've actually written a small book, *Clean Your Room: An Out-Of-The-Box Manual*, for helping people look at their lifestyle and finding ways to achieve the goal of purity. Healthy reversals are the natural way of life. They're supposed to happen. If we are effectively wearing dirty diapers, we are not privy to what otherwise would be our birthright: Divine assistance to turn negative circumstances around without so much heavy lifting. Try it.

Resistance

I wrote about this topic on Quora, a website where people ask questions and experts answer questions. I got a lot of pushback on my answer about whether therapists should swear. Of course, I feel nobody should swear but especially not people who are functioning in the role of elders. It wasn't a popular response. People don't like anyone telling them what they can and can't say. Especially a therapist. That a therapist would think to give feedback like this to a client sounded preachy. So I specified the way the topic might look if it came up:

> Let's say this client is so frustrated. Every guy she dates is worse than the last one. Treats her badly. Selfish. There was an interesting teaching given over by Caroline Myss in a lecture. She effectively paraphrases the ideas we find in mystical texts. There are three levels of people which she calls *eau d'toilet*, cologne and perfume. Like the Olympics: bronze, silver and gold. Myss conjectures that people choose their level. She suggests that people will find friends at their own level, a job at that level and a partner at that same level.
>
> If there is truth to this (an idea we looked at in an earlier chapter) and somebody believes that they are dating people at a lower level than they would wish, the question becomes how they can raise their level so that they warrant attracting a higher caliber, less base or selfish partner.

I added, "I'm not saying something foreign in our culture. People already understand, 'dress for the job that you want to get.' So what I'm talking about is another version of what contemporary psychologist Jordan Peterson talks about when he says "clean your room." I continued:

> Not everybody uses profanity. If you want to upgrade, if you want to attract a higher level partner, maybe changes in speech patterns is one way to implement a standard and thereby broadcast that you cast your sights high in terms of the quality that you wish to attract.

It's amazing to me that people want to preserve impurity in speech yet, if somebody walked out in public with food all over their teeth, stains all over their clothes and messy hair, all would perceive this the kiss of death in terms of getting a job or a date. Yet using profanity, the auditory equivalent of negativity, is perceived as a necessary expression of free speech! Something is wrong here.

> Linguist Kate Burridge notes that over the years English has accumulated more than 2500 expressions for the procreative organs.

And Now a Word from Our Sponsor . . .

One passage of the Hebrew Bible is relevant here: Deuteronomy 23, 13-15. The Israelite soldiers are given specific directions how to conduct themselves in the circumstance of war. The text advises:

> You shall have a place outside the camp, and to it you shall go out. You shall have a shovel in addition to your weapons, and it will be that when you sit outside, you shall dig with it; you shall go back and cover your excrement. For your G-d walks in the midst of your camp to rescue you and to deliver your enemies before you; so your camp shall be holy, so that He will not see a shameful thing among you and turn away from behind you.

Note the claim here: that Divinity picks up and leaves in the presence of excrement. No more Divine intervention or assistance. Not what you would want to hear when you are on the battle field! Enough to motivate your average Israelite soldier to carry a shovel!

Another idea to reflect on. The association to the "4 letter word" in Jewish vernacular is the most sacred name associated with Divinity, a name so sacred Jews are not to utter it. When we think of the concept of the "4 letter word" in secular society, you know what comes up! What's the problem here? And whatever the problem is, are you sure you want to be a mouthpiece for it.

In summary, we see that humor can catapult us to another level, literally escorting us to a very special albeit short visit to the world of unity. Imagine, if we all worked on our speech, if we improved and hosted more clarity and purity, how much more we could achieve! Imagine if the humor we enjoyed avoided crude language instead of steeping us in that which is base!

It's a messianic vision! Not just that people would talk better to each other, they would talk better to themselves. The messages they gave themselves would be more positive and hopeful. There would be more insight, less reactivity, more laughter. What if we each got to higher levels in terms of how we articulate ourselves? A brighter future is potentially near at hand.

9.

Building a Mansion in the Sky

I wonder if you have heard the story of 7-Up, a drink which, at one time, was the 4rth most popular soda in the United States. You may not know: 7-Up was brought to market 6 times under 6 different names and, each time, failed to garner market share. The 7th time it was brought out yet again, put forward with the name we know well. Why '7-Up?'? There were 7 discrete ingredients in this product. Somehow, this name shot the product to fame and popularity. Go figure.

Could Kabbalah conjecture about that success? In the mystical model, The Tree of Life, from Genesis fame, was more than a tree. The mystical tradition asserts that that Tree was/is a conceptual model of reality, G-d and even self. Every self. Specifically, the model has 10 'Divine Attributes', attributes that are also ours because we are made in the image of our Creator (as per Genesis). The 10 Attributes break into two divisions: 3 Attributes associated with the higher world and 7 Attributes, lower, associate with the physical world.

As a result of this demarcation, the number 7 has everything to do with the physical world. There are 7 colors in the rainbow, 7 notes in the musical scale (the 8th is a repetition), 7 days of the week, 7 aspects associated with space (6 directions and the center point with connects them). The body has 4 limbs, one head, torso and the hidden element, the soul, all which adds up to seven. We live in the domain of the seven.

What is our task, mystically put? To raise the domain of seven, the concrete physical world, elevating it to the higher octave, associated with the number 3. Our task is to strive upward, to lift the physical by living in accordance with higher principles that come from above. We are to do "7-Up."

I'd like to suggest that we intrinsically know our task is to elevate the domain of 7, so when a soda comes along with that name, it twigs us. We buy it.

Another interesting thing about that soda, by the way: it was always marketed with distinctively 'spiritual' imagery. Commercials told us, "It was, is and always will be the leading soda." The image of a man chugging down clear soda, as he props the bottle overhead and drinks with his head inclined back. The mystic sees the Divine waters, another symbol of Heaven's bounty, coming down from above. Is it possible that marketers are aware of certain images that represent foundational ideas, ideas that we harbor on an unconscious level?

Regardless of the answer, which we obviously cannot say for certain, I'd like to suggest that the image of Mary flinging her beret upward, part of the imagery that we watched on the Mary Tyler Moore Show as the credits rolled, was a meaningful gesture, relative to our agenda as articulated by the mystical tradition. We are here to lift the physical world, the zone of the 7, to transcend it, to morph the world which often presents us with 'nothing' days. We are charged with the task of making those nothing days into something worthwhile.

How will we do that? Sometimes a funny word, a joke, a burst of creativity can do a world of good dealing with the tensions of life. In so doing, you are taking the physical world, the concrete aspects of the world associated with the number seven, and elevating it; reaching out of the world of limitation and thrusting upward towards infinity.

That's what you achieve when you remove the negativity from your life, do a remake on your speech patterns, making yourself a vessel for light. You brighten up, your life and that of those around you, simply by virtue of how you choose to articulate. Of course, living in a moral and kind way is another way to raise the physical to loftier heights. Let's though, take one more spin, to get more clarity about what it means to live in the higher plane, not just go for a brief visit, courtesy of an entertainer or witty friend. We have to explore the mystical concept of the Mansion.

The Mansion

There's an interesting idea in the world of religious studies: if you want to understand a concept better, find the first place you see that concept mentioned in the Bible. That first mention provides subtle insight into the nature of the phenomenon in question.

Case in point. What is a question? If you read the Hebrew Bible you can search out the first question. Adam and Eve have eaten the forbidden fruit and, guilty in their sin, they run into the forest to 'hide'. G-d seems to play along. He says, and here comes the first question: "Where are you?" Surely He knows where they are. So what's with the question?

Let's look under the metaphysical hood: According to Jewish mystical sources, reality as we know it is comprised of four different worlds. The lowest world, called the 'World of Action," is characterized by physicality which we experience through our senses. The 3 higher worlds are spiritual in nature. The dimensions of these worlds are abstract.

In the World of Action, the concept of space takes the form of physical place, the landscape, the background or context where life occurs. In the higher worlds space manifests differently and has a different name: "mansion."

A mansion is a framework which defines relationships, a network of associations, between forms, beings, ideas or other variables. A mansion harbors schemas which establish how various aspects of existence relate to each other. The mansion can contain a rich network of associations, can be populated by disorganized and haphazard associations, can be empty and vacuous; there are countless permutations (Steinsaltz, 2006).

When people properly inhabit the higher worlds they will have more elaborate mansions. In that case, the physical world holds less sway. Such people are less effected by happenings in the lowest world, the World of Action, and have an easier time resisting temptation. Their life map, their mansion, is their anchor.

How does this play out in life? Imagine one individual whose mansion is relatively sparse. When faced with day to day temptations, he easily falls. Without an anchor in the higher worlds, without a sophisticated worldview that activates his highest motives and rivets him to worthwhile goals, he suffers the pressures of day-to-day existence and succumbs to cravings. Compare this to another person who has a rich web of associations regarding loyalties, faith, the meaning of life, values, priorities, a relationship with the Divine, etc. This individual, anchored in an extensive network of thoughts, understandings, values, relationships and visions, is less attached to the world of physicality and more easily resists temptation.

Donny Osmond vs. Michael Jackson

When I was young, I followed the teen idols of the day. One family, The Osmonds, were well known, a group of singing brothers and a sister. The Osmonds were committed Mormons. Another family musical group, The Jackson 5, were also popular during the same years.

I've been thinking about the Osmonds because the siblings, now in their sixties, are coming through the YouTube feed. Their children and grandchildren have assembled videos, a montage of family photos documenting the legacy of long-standing marriages. What is the secret sauce that has former teen idol Donny Osmond enjoying his grandchildren while superstar Michael Jackson is dead, felled years ago by a drug overdose?

Using the frame we are discussing here, I would say that Donny Osmond's mansion was more robust. Osmond himself says that family has been the most important thing in his life. We know that his mansion, characterized by the value of family and faith, has served as a powerful anchor.

'Where Are You?' Revisited

So this takes us back to the question, "where are you?" That question is not about the patently obvious: "Well, I'm standing right next to you at the checkout counter" or in the case of Adam, "I'm sitting under this oak tree." The question targets where you live in the continuum of the four worlds. Do you have a well-nourished mansion which anchors you to a higher world, having subjugated the world of physicality? Do you have a philosophy that guides you, or values that direct you? Or are you detached from the higher worlds and mired in the lowest world, the world of physicality, leaving you subject to the storms of the day? Where are you?

For the commentators, "Where are you?" is the first question in the Torah because this question is the first and ultimate life question. It's the question that matters. We need to get our bearings. If we have cultivated a mansion up above, we have a rich set of associations. We said the upper world is the world of unity, the place where everything is ultimately connected to every other thing, albeit the pathway of connection may be unusual, relative to day-to-day standards. The funnier we are, the more we have developed the mansion. The more we see a complex network of associations. The more we are girded by spiritual values, the more we inhabit the mansion.[1]

When Mary's beret stands suspended up in space in the opening credits of that show, I would suggest that we see a graphic representation of the mansion of our protagonist, Mary Richards. Mary had one foot firmly girded in the higher heights: in classical values that anchored her, committing her to a standard of grace and providing leverage dealing with difficult characters and scenarios. For Mary, the performer, she discussed a life replete with many, many losses, including that of her son at a young age. Just know: whether we, in our lives, are contending with daily work conundrums or devastating losses, having a well-furnished mansion is going to help us cope. Mary role modeled the possession of this mansion, girding herself to classical values and standards of speech and behavior, something that we, too, could hope to achieve.

---

1. Of course, we have noted that some people can be very funny but NOT girded by spiritual values, and what can result is toxic humor. In one sense, the have a mansion with many associations, but in another sense, the mansion is impoverished.

The 'Shen'

Hebrew letter: Shin

I've mentioned several letters of the Hebrew alphabet. Now I'd like to add to the collection. Here we have pictured a letter called *Shin*. This letter looks like a fire; we see flames leaping up and more specifically, the letter represents the Divine spark of each person. The sound associated with this letter: *sh*. The sound of fire.

There is fire in our constitutions. When the *Hey* lands, it is like a breathe of air (the *H* sound) which stokes the inner fire, just as bellows can flame the fire in a hearth. The Tree of Life suggests this Hebrew letter occupies a place in the chest of each person. The Chinese tradition teaches that the 'Wild Birds of *Shen*' are the facets of the soul which specifically motor the heart and its meridian. And the Chinese refer to the 'heart-mind' as the *Xin*. I'd like to suggest that different traditions are talking about the same concepts, same real estate, whether referring to the *Shin*, the *Shen* or the *Xin*.

When we are self-possessed, evolved, centered, we are operating in a balanced way where we can access feelings and the mind simultaneously. We won't fall into decisions driven only by the senses or only by the intellect. Some traditions call this place of selfhood 'wise mind'.

From this vantage point, new approaches to dealing with problems can land. When you live centered in this place, you are more 'elegant than elephant', as the saying goes. And this is the self you animate when you are clever and witty, reaching into conceptualizations from the world of unity, melting what could be an uncomfortable moment with just the right light comment.

We can be clever when we inhabit the mansion, we can be moral, we can love and be loved. We must keep our sights high, knowing that the quest for humor can point us upward to a state that has euphoric feelings *and* transcendent values awaiting us there. Of course, this is the problem with comedians today. They inhabit a realm of multiple associations, but fail to populate the mansion with wholesome values that can elevate.

Reflect that in Hebrew, the word for teeth are *shinayim*. The expression of the *Shen, Shin* or *Xin* occurs with the aid of the teeth, hence a word for teeth which alludes to the *Shin*. We define our moral heights by what we say (and how we eat). The higher self emerges, or not, based on the choices we make when we articulate. How to light the world up with your smile? The teeth have it! Careful how you use them!

Keep your eye on the prize. What starts as a quest for a laugh becomes, in the end, a journey to the destination of joy, itself. Settle for no less! And your access, I would suggest, is a value: to prioritize purity and so prepare for lift-off. No need to drag yourself through the gutter. Uplift your language, rectify your humor and uplift your life. It's time to build, it's time to fortify your mansion in the sky.

10.

Make Your Life a Comedy

Lots of challenges these days. Psychologist Jordan Peterson has advice: make your life a comedy

In this book, we have been revisiting *The Mary Tyler Moore Show* & *Rhoda* where you will find classic Jewish humor. Can our reflections on these shows help direct us. How might we make our lives a comedy?

Peterson explains his advice in the following way: "you want to be presented with a problem [as occurs in a comedy], you want the problem to take you apart and you want the problem to put you together in a better way." He means that in comedies the protagonist is faced with a challenge that exceeds his or her capacity to succeed. Ultimately, by retooling, our hero reforms and now is able to manage the task. The ending is happy.

That needs to be you.

Comedy writer Steve Epstein puts it another way: "Comedy is about an ordinary guy struggling against insurmountable odds without many of the required skills and tools with which to win, yet never giving up hope."

Yes! Let that be us!

Can we learn from Mary? Can she help you make your life a comedy?

You bet! But first! A segue – believe it or not – to Genesis.

In Genesis, we read:

> and a river flows from Eden to water the garden; from there it divides and becomes four major rivers. (Genesis, 2, 10)

Rabbi Chaim Kramer cites an interpretation of this line: the single source dividing into four alludes to the composition of this world; a single source element divides into the four elements. Everything in the world is composed of water, air, fire and earth in an endless array of combinations. When the elements are bound, one with the other, there is life; when the elements disperse, death. The single source is the life force that binds the disparate elements together.

What is the single source that imbues life? The answer: the *tzaddik*, the righteous elder, the sage. The four elements, each with properties that are radically different from the others, will fall into disharmony unless they continue to receive life force from the *tzaddik*.

The *Likutey Halakhot* states that while all people are comprised of all four elements, each person has a root in one particular element and possesses character traits that derive from that element. Given all our intrinsic differences, the capacity exists for terrible strife. In fact, without a harmonizing force, strife is the norm, resulting in conflict and chaos.

"The controlling force which can harmonize these differences," states this text, "is the single source element, the *tzaddik*. The *tzaddik* knows how to establish a proper balance between the various elements in his domain" (*Likutey Halakhot, Matzranut* 4:1-3 as quoted in Kramer, 1998). Or in our case, the *tzaddik* knows how to establish a proper balance between the various personalities in the community.

Back to Mary. Each character on that show struggled with one – or more – of the 'deadly sins'. Rhoda: eternally envious of the beautiful Mary. Lou Grant: an angry bully, a drinker, an over-eater. Ted Baxter's pride knew no limits. Sue Ann Nivins: driven by lust and pride. Murray Slaughter discharged his anger issues via an ongoing stream of passive-aggressive insults.

In other words, all the people in that show were . . . like us! Full of flaws, given over to excesses, prone to conflict.

Phyllis hated Rhoda. Ted was a trigger for Murray and Lou; Sue Ann, for Murray and the feeling was mutual. Then you had Mary, modulated, driven by the urge to be good, to make things good, to see the good in the broken people around her.

Mary: the harmonizer, ignoring provocation, then, in some moments, setting limits; in others, registered the lunacy around her. Mary played it straight and conflicts became fodder for laughs. That show was a Jewish morality play! We could all stand to learn from Mary Richards or, for that matter, from Mary Tyler Moore, herself.

She, who, in a certain sense, stood at the helm of the women's liberation movement, in terms of how much she achieved professionally, how many women she employed. At the same time, she refused a role in social activism instead fundraising for her causes (diabetes research and animal welfare). Of course. her lead attribute: a quiet grace. Here's a quote that is attributed to her:

I live in a type of controlled awareness. I wouldn't call it fear, but it's an awareness. I know I have an obligation to behave in a certain way. And I am able to do that.

Want to be a harmonizer? There is a quiet technology to master. As you architect the new you, channel Mary!

She who is mindful of her impact, cautious in her dealings, calibrated, allows others to shine their light, full of their idiosyncrasies, creates environments where humor emerges, dwarfing judgement, the more usual currency in our social universe. Emulate the one who immortalized the trait of Grace in a medium that would, in a few short years, abandon reverence and traditional values, altogether. Fifty years later, put the hours you spent watching Mary – in your formative years – to good use. Make your life a comedy.[1]

1. Reprinted with permission from the Times of Israel blog.

11.

Revisiting "Knock, Knock"

In 1987, Psychologist Francine Shapiro, out for a walk, had an interesting awareness. A negative thought had popped into her mind and then, by happenstance, her eyes flitted back and forth, from the right to the left and back, and she noticed a change in her thinking pattern. Curious, she registered her change of mood, change of feeling. She decided to research and explore if others noticed that the back-and-forth motion of the eyes seemed to neutralize the negativity of thoughts or memories. The rest, as they say, is history.

At this point in time, Eye Movement Desensitization Reprocessing (EMDR) is one of the most studied and seemingly effective techniques for working with trauma. Over time, it became clear that the technique involved bilateral brain stimulation. What started as an eye movement technique now has practitioners handing clients hand probes which vibrate, first one, then the other. Each probe is held in one or the other hand. Another means of performing this technique: through headphones. Music or soft beeps can alternate from one earpiece to the other. Patients are involved in specific imagery while undergoing this process. Research has determined the therapeutic value of this technique without determining exactly why this technique seems to work.

Kabbalah, of course, would have its answer. Holding the opposites, doing an action that replicates what we understand as the spiritual anatomy ("male and female, He created them"), the back-and-forth moving from one polarity to the other, shoots us out into a more expansive frame of mind. It's the reversal! It's the duality: "Knock, Knock!" One knock is *Yin*. The other is *Yang*. EMDR, then, is sending us to the same altitude we visit when we have a good laugh. We shoot outside of our problems and perspectives. We go further afield. Above it all. We take a little hypnotic sojourn.

"Go to Yourself"

Speaking of a sojourn, let's remember a section of the Torah that relates to Abraham. If you know the Hebrew, that section begins with the following Hebrew words: *Lech lecha*. Those two words are effectively the same Hebrew letters, same two words ("Knock, Knock"), only the punctuation changes the meaning. The first word means "Go!" The second word means, "to yourself!" There it is. The line effectively reads "Go to yourself, to the land I'm going to show you, leave the land of your father. . . ." This issue is from G-d, Himself and relates not only to *Avram*. It relates to each one of us.

We are all to leave the 'land of our father', the neuroses we grew up with, the energetic pattering we acquired in childhood. We are sent forth. "*Lech lecha*"! Go! Where? To *Yang–Yin*. To the proper balance of the masculine and feminine polarity which can only be achieved by leaving your personal neurotic structure initially shaped within the family of origin, stepping out of issues that tug you back there. "Move on. Take leave. Get over it."

The call to Abraham is a call to the hero's journey. It's an invitation to that which is therapeutic, having a person revisit the choreography of masculine/feminine that is their birthright and brings them back into proper formation so they are true to their point of origin: they were, after all, made 'in the image of the Divine': masculine and feminine! By leaving home, a person is privy to other perspectives, other worldviews, more objectivity, more influence of the ideas from new people you have yet to meet. Who knows what and who you will encounter in that distant land.

Knock, Knock. Indeed.

Laughing at Yourself

No wonder we must be able to laugh at ourselves! It means we have left the home of the father, stopped taking our issues quite so seriously, played with different vantage points. Laughter and therapy have a lot in common. In my opinion, there should be more efforts to cross pollinate these two. When we do so, we, as therapists (or friends who want to help our friends or whatever the relationship), are assuming the role of trickster. Caroline Casey has a lot to say about that interesting archetype. The trickster is the character who can help us "throw old vows into the cauldron and ladle out new ones," says Casey. She tells us that the trickster turns a mirror into a window ("look, how beautiful!"), then into a door. Then says to us, "follow me! Let's go!"

How to Turn Breakdown into Breakthrough

I'm actually going to suggest that we need to get more acuity so we can see the internal infrastructure that is our own. We are meant to hold ourselves up and determine the nature of our imbalances. Am I too *Yin*? Too static, detail-oriented, perfectionistic? Am I too *Yang*? Too all over the place, too ADD, lacking concentration skills? In fact, there are so many permutations, so many ways that we can manifest our imbalances and these become the key for understanding where we are relative to the internal pattern that is focal for many spiritual frameworks.

The first step is popping into the euphoric state associated with new learning and finding new perspectives. Go have a laugh! And from there, go further afield. Learn something new! Change things up! Take a comedy improvisation course! Learn a new language! Get dancing lessons! Assume new choreography so you can work towards becoming more fluid, divining down the *Qi* in a plentiful way that improves your health and mood. *Tai Chi* anyone?

The State of Progress

When you laugh, you surrender to a bodily experience. You can't talk while you laugh. You marinate in a type of receptivity, this alongside a group of people, most of whom you don't know. In the end, the laughter project moves us out of everyday existence. Now, we explore a different state, characterized by unity: with others, bathing in pleasant hormones, releasing worries associated with day-to-day life. That's where this whole project is leading. That is how, therefore, I need to end:

The Silent Teacher

Though the *Tai Ji* may sound unfamiliar, you have certainly seen it. That ancient Eastern symbol, depicting *Yin & Yang*, two primal energies that permeate our world, is seen on T-shirts and in health-care ads. Embedded in that symbol are layers of teachings savored by mystics and physicists alike. But what you may not know is that Judaism has its own *Tai Ji*, a symbol that contains similar teachings about the dualities of this world. Allow me to introduce the letter, *Aleph*.

The numerical value of that letter is the number one, representing the One above. Yet, Rabbi Yitzchak Ginsburgh teaches that the Hebrew word "*Aleph*" is also associated with the number 1000 since that word shares a root with *Aleph*. *Aleph* therefore represents both unity and multiplicity; the one tree with thousands of leaves; one human body with millions of neurons. Psychologically, *Aleph* reminds us that besides being the star of our own lives we are each, also, one small cell in the cosmic body of all humanity, that being the central paradox of existence.

According to the mystics, the Hebrew letters were created and then used as the building blocks of all subsequent creations. *Aleph* the first letter, was a firstborn, so to speak Given its favorable placement, you might expect a letter with attitude. But no, *Aleph* has a decidedly low-profile. Unlike the other letters, it has no sound. Says Richard Seidman,

> "*Aleph* is the sound that comes before sound. *Aleph* is so close to the divine essence, on the edge of the holy nothingness from which sound and form emerge, that it can't be constrained within a particular sound. We "pronounce" *Aleph* by opening our mouths but saying nothing, as if we were speechless with awe and wonder."

And how are we to resolve that paradox? The form of *Aleph*, a diagonal line with a comma attached above and below, represents the duality of creation. Above is the upper world, the heavens, and below is our earthly world. Our task is to walk the line of connection, to bridge the gap between two disparate realities and to embrace both worlds, both sides of life.

Aleph, then, gives us the big picture, and addresses a perceptual problem described by Albert Einstein who wrote,

> "A human being is part of a whole, called by us the Universe, a part limited in time and space. He experiences himself, his thoughts and feelings, as something separated from the rest — a kind of optical delusion of his consciousness. This delusion is a kind of prison for us, restricting us to our personal desires and . . . to affection for a few persons nearest us. Our task must be to free ourselves from this prison"

In Jane Wagner's one-woman play, *The Search for Intelligent Life in This Universe*, Trudy, a bag lady, is befriended by Martians who seek to learn about humanity on our planet. Trudy takes her space chums on a tour and their final destination is the back of a packed theater, standing in the dark while a one-woman show comes to a close. Says Trudy,

> " . . . all of a sudden I feel one of 'em tug my sleeve, whispers, "Trudy, look." I said, "Yeah, goose bumps. You definitely got goose bumps. You really like the play that much?" They said it wasn't the play gave 'em goose bumps, it was the audience. I forgot to tell 'em to watch the play; they'd been watching the audience! Yeah, to see a group of strangers sitting together in the dark, laughing and crying about the same things . . . that just knocked 'em out."

When we leave our solitary prisons once and for all, I think we will all have goose bumps. In the meantime, let's let *Aleph* lead the way by helping us cultivate an appreciation of the oneness of all and so bridging the gap between worlds, between people and between nations. Ironic, though it is, the world was created by the spoken word but its perfection will be achieved only through attending the sounds of silence, rendering us all speechless, all one.

Bibliography

Feldman, David (1986). *Imponderables: The Solution to the Mysteries of Everyday Life*. New York: W. Morrow.

Feldman, David (1991). *Do Penguins Have Knees?* New York: HarperCollins.

Feldman, David (1992). *When Did Wild Poodles Roam the Earth?* New York: HarperCollins.

Fisher, Carrie (1987). *Postcards from the Edge*. New York: Simon and Schuster.

Ginsburgh, Yitzchak (2006). *What You Need to Know about Kabbalah*. Brooklyn, NY: Dwelling Place Publishing.

Haley, Jay (1993). *Uncommon Therapy: The Psychiatric Techniques of Milton H Erickson*. New York: W.W. Norton.

Hillman, James & Ventura, Michael (1993). *We've had a Hundred Years of Psychotherapy and the World is Getting Worse*. New York: HarperSanFrancisco.

Hillman, James (1999). *The Force of Character and the Lasting Life*. New York: Random House.

Jacobson, YY, Rabbi. *The Purpose of Life is to Generate Laugher*, Part 1. YouTube.

Jacobson, YY, Rabbi. *The Purpose of Life is to Generate Laugher*, Part 2. YouTube.

Osmond, Marie & Wilkie, Marcia (2009). *Might as Well Laugh about it Now*. New York: Thorndike Press.

Popcorn, Faith & Marigold, Lys (1996). *10 Trends to Future Fit your Life, Your Work, and Your Business*. New York: HarperCollins.

Puett, Michael and Gross-Loh, Christine (2016). *The Path: What Chinese Philosophers Can Teach Us about Living the Good Life*. New York: Simon & Shuster

Schneider, Sarah (2001). *Kabbalistic Writings on the Nature of Masculine & Feminine*. New Jersey: Jason Aronson

Seidman, Richard (2001). *The Oracle of Kabbalah*. New York: St. Martin's Press.

Steinsaltz, Adin (2003). *Opening the Tanya: Discovering the Moral & Mystical Teachings of a Classic Work of Kabbalah*. San Francisco: Jossey Bass.

Steinsaltz, Adin (2006). *The Thirteen Petaled Rose*. Northvale, New York: Basic Books.

Stone Edition (2001). *The Chumash*. Brooklyn, New York: Mesorah Publications.

Tatz, Akiva (1993). *Living Inspired*. Southfield, Michigan: Targum Press.

Tatz, Akiva (1995). *Worldmask*. Southfield, Michigan: Targum Press.

Zhiming, Yuan (2010). *Tao Te Ching; Original Text and a Modern Interpretation* (Translated by Daniel Baida Su and Chen Shangyu). Bloomington, IN: AuthorHouse.

Next Steps

Want to learn more about Kabbalah? The following book is available as an e-book:

Reading the Soul: Kabbalah & the Psychology of Handwriting

By Annette Poizner, MSW, Ed.D.

Can Kabbalah help us understand our unique and individual personalities? Can our handwriting help us see through to the core of who we are and who we could be? Annette Poizner suggests that the ancient Tree of Life and the European discipline of clinical graphology can provide self insight; also can help us see a unique structure that pervades creation, serving as DNA that undergirds our world and our psyches, helping us to understand who we are and how we need to develop.

In this book, Poizner traces the imprint of Divinity on creation. Exploring the nooks and crannies of our world – surveying diverse areas including graphic design, cultural norms, marketing practices, handedness and more – allows us to see unity, the watermark of Divinity, at the root of creation. As we explore the central pattern at play, we delve into a visual adventure: learning the structure of Divinity by analyzing the handwriting of public figures..

Poizner, author of *Clinical Graphology: An Interpretive Manual for Mental Health Practitioners*, introduces Graphology, a bona fide

European technique, to illustrate how the template of Divinity is our first and only nature. Learning about Oprah, Streisand, Deepak Chopra and others, you will learn about yourself! Explore the profound truths about self and soul that flow each time you pick up a pen . . . en route to our ultimate destination, not to know the rich and famous, but to know G-d and Self. As Poizner writes, "If the Divine infrastructure is intrinsically relevant to us, then societal disinterest in G-d not only banishes G-d but, in some sense, ourselves. We may not know who, or how, to be." .

In a work 15 years in the making, Poizner weaves together the ideas of Jewish Mysticism, Chinese medical theory and Jungian psychology, to survey the interior of our world from a most unique vantage point.

Other books in this series:

Kabbalah Café: Ancient Wisdom for Modern Minds

By Annette Poizner, MSW, Ed.D.

The Kabbalah Café is a collection of essays which trace the relevance of Jewish mystical concepts to contemporary life, exploring themes that pervade our daily existence, providing a mystical perspective on area that are commonly considered the domain of psychology, philosophy or medicine. Topics include the nature of self-esteem and identity, insights into psycho-physical phenomena such as anger, sadness, fear, worry, laughter, pain and pleasure, and ideas about our various sensory modalities and the structure of the body. According to the mystics, the latter two realms reveal higher truths about the hidden structure of the world. When applicable, scientific findings, clinical anecdotes or concepts that come from other wisdom traditions will be cited, providing soft support for a mystical worldview that asserts that one truth pervades reality. The ideas in these essays are designed to introduce a worldview that registers a rich bandwidth of reality beyond the one we normally see. Brought to you by an author who is a voracious reader, seasoned psychotherapist and trained observer of human behavior, prepare to see with fresh eyes – a dose of what she calls Vitamin See – leading you on a path home, to the address of the Inner I.

This work is inspired by Christopher Phillips' *Socrates Café*, which introduced the relevance of concepts from classical philosophy to everyday life. I aspire to bring mystical perspectives to readers, showing how ancient wisdom can inform and deepen our lives.

Available as a print book and in digital format.

"Knock, Knock": The Kabbalah of Comedy

By Annette Poizner, MSW, Ed.D.

Laughter: a double edged sword. Positive humor engenders euphoria; negative, seeds humiliation. Triggered by the COVID quarantine, Therapist and Author Annette Poizner revisited the sitcoms of her youth – the Mary Tyler Moore Show and Rhoda. Looking through the lens of the ancient Kabbalah, Poizner, then, performed an inquiry into laughter, examining the mystical infrastructure of this every day phenomenon and getting insight into the how, why and what of funny.

Can we find the root of all humor in the 'Knock, Knock' jokes of yesteryear? Or even further back, with the 'Peekabo' we play when interacting with babies? What is the reversal that characterizes the punchline of a joke? Does that reversal correspond with other aspects of day-to-day life? Where do we go when we laugh and what can we learn from that destination – about ourselves, life and transcendence?

Reaching into mystical teachings, we will find a frame that allows us to understand Mary Tyler Moore and her unique accomplishments, as well as the women's movement and its place in the cosmic dance between Masculine and Feminine, a dance that has its origins in Genesis. The humor of a handful of funny Jews who brought Mary, Rhoda and friends to life will provide fodder, letting us analyze and access the Divinity that rests at the core of the laughter mechanism.

We'll consider how to prime that mechanism, ensuring its optimal and healthy use, reducing toxic forms of laughter and helping readers access the inner mansion, a world of unity which makes life funny – but also meaningful. In what promises to be an expose in an area of life rarely unpacked for its hidden meaning and metaphor, join the author for a look behind the screen, pun intended. What starts as a quest for euphoria leads us simultaneously on a journey to self, to the oceanic consciousness where everything connects to everything and finally, to nothing at all, your ultimate and best destination. Who knew all of this and more occurs in that ephemeral moment when a punchline does its thing.

Annette Poizner, MSW, Ed.D. RSW

Annette Poizner is a therapist in private practice, a published author and community educator. She completed her Social Work graduate degree at Columbia University of New York and a Doctorate in Education (specializing in Counseling Psychology) at the University of Toronto.

She has specialized training in techniques developed by Dr. Milton Erickson, as well as advanced training in the use of Eye Movement Desensitization Reprocessing (EMDR) and Neuro Linguistic Programming (NLP). She is the co-founder of the Milton H. Erickson Institute of Toronto and founded and chaired the Jewish Health Alliance, a continuing education organization which explored the intersection between Judaism and the healing arts over the course of 10 years.

Her work had been featured in dailies across Canada, in trade magazines across North America, and in clinical and academic venues such as at the Canadian Psychological Association annual conference and other professional meetings. She is the author of a textbook published by a leading scholarly publishing house. She has recently published several volumes relating to the work and teachings of Dr. Jordan Peterson, having found areas where his work resonates with ideas found within the Jewish mystical tradition.

You can read more about her work on her blog on Medium.com. Her YouTube channel link is here. She also answers questions, as time permits, on Quora.com. To be advised of the release of the next book in this series or to contact her with feedback about this work (which will be sporadically updated) please email ap@annettepoizner.com. You can visit her store at https://macrourl.com/annettestore.

Other Works by This Author

Kabbalah Café: Ancient Wisdom for Modern Minds

The Kabbalah Café is a collection of essays which trace the relevance of Jewish mystical concepts to contemporary life, exploring themes that pervade our daily existence, providing a mystical perspective on area that are commonly considered the domain of psychology, philosophy or medicine.

Topics include the nature of self-esteem and identity, insights into psycho-physical phenomena such as anger, sadness, fear, worry, laughter, pain and pleasure, and ideas about our various sensory modalities and the structure of the body. According to the mystics, the latter two realms reveal higher truths about the hidden structure of the world.

When applicable, scientific findings, clinical anecdotes or concepts that come from other wisdom traditions will be cited, providing soft support for a mystical worldview that asserts that one truth pervades reality. The ideas in these essays are designed to introduce a worldview that registers a rich bandwidth of reality beyond the one we normally see. Brought to you by an author who is a voracious reader, seasoned therapist and trained observer of human behavior, prepare to see with fresh eyes – a dose of what she calls Vitamin See – leading you on a path home, to the address of the Inner I.

This work is inspired by Christopher Phillips' Socrates Café, which introduced the relevance of concepts from classical philosophy to everyday life. I aspire to bring mystical perspectives to readers, showing how ancient wisdom can inform and deepen our lives.

Lobster University Press

I have dedicated myself to unpacking the rich work of Dr. Jordan Peterson because I find massive overlap between the ideas he expresses and the teachings of the ancient Kabbalah. Here you can read about the various works I have prepared, some to summarize and explain his core ideas, others to show the correspondence between his concepts and those of Kabbalah. For those works which discuss Kabbalistic ideas in detail, look for the asterisk.

A Practical Summary & Workbook for Using Jordan Peterson's 'Maps of Meaning' to Sort Yourself Out

Less Chaos, More Order!

Finding Jordan Peterson's "Maps of Meaning: The Architecture of Belief" difficult to follow? Curious to learn more about the man and his ideas? This summary reviews some of the core insights that characterize Peterson's worldview. Love him or hate him, you might as well get to the crux of what he is saying, particularly as it relates to self-improvement and personal development! With a seasoned psychotherapist as your guide, access Peterson's premises about the nature of reality and how we best live within it. Summaries, summaries of the summaries and reflection points to journal, help you digest teachings so you can apply them to your day-to-day life. The second part of this book introduces Alfred Adler's technique for decoding the 'map of meaning' by analyzing a person's 10 earliest memories, further demonstrating how that map manifests in the lives of individuals. This hands-on workbook helps you access vintage Peterson, here presented in a linear style – minus mythology or brain science – so you can zero in on the life advice that has helped many achieve dramatic personal change.

Volume 2
An Illustrated Guide for Using Jordan Peterson's Insights on Divinity & the Map of Meaning to Sort Yourself Out*

By Annette Poizner, MSW, Ed.D., RSW

According to Dr. Jordan Peterson, secular society has overlooked the psychological importance of Divinity, failing to understand the template it provides that helps us flourish. If Peterson is right, we need to review what classic texts tell us about the intricate and specific structure of the G-dhead. Lo and behold, that exact structure pervades creation, serving as DNA that undergirds the physical world, the human body, the contours of the psyche and more.

In this book, Annette Poizner, a therapist, first explores Peterson's insights about Divinity, then traces the imprint of Divinity on creation. Exploring the nooks and crannies of our world – surveying diverse areas including graphic design, cultural norms, marketing practices, handedness and more – allows us to see unity, the watermark of Divinity, at the root of creation. As we explore the central pattern at play, we delve into a visual adventure: learning the structure of Divinity by – believe it or not – analyzing the handwriting of public figures.

Poizner introduces Clinical Graphology, a bona fide European technique for assessing personality, to illustrate how the template of Divinity is our first and only nature. Learning about Oprah, Streisand, Deepak Chopra and others, you will learn about yourself! Explore the profound truths about self and soul that flow each time you pick up a pen . . . en route to our ultimate destination, not to know the rich and famous, but to know G-d and Self. As Poizner writes, "If the Divine infrastructure is intrinsically relevant to us, then societal disinterest and abandonment of the G-d ideal not only banishes G-d but, in some sense, ourselves. We may not know who, or how, to be." Of course, this is exactly Peterson's point.

In a work 15 years in the making, Poizner weaves together the ideas of Jordan Peterson, Jewish Mysticism, Chinese medical theory, Jungian psychology, and 30 years of clinical experience, to survey the interior of our world from a most unique vantage point.

Volume 3
This Way Up: A Faith-Based Introduction to Jordan Peterson's 'Maps of Meaning'*

By Annette Poizner, MSW, Ed.D., RSW

Jordan Peterson's books are selling furiously, widely cited in the media and part of an ongoing conversation. This book addresses why those in the faith-based communities should familiarize themselves with this work. Psychotherapist Annette Poizner argues that Peterson's work is awakening the hearts and minds of a generation, prompting an army of young people to question the premises of secularism and ponder the tenets of faith. In this zeitgeist, clergy and laypeople are better equipped to address the needs of young people walking through their doors if they understand the worldview Peterson is advancing. This book is designed to summarize some of Peterson's important concepts including his ideas about the nature of reality and its constituent aspects, the structure of the mind, and the psychological necessity of the G-d ideal. These ideas will be presented through the lens of faith, referring to teachings which are drawn from a detailed study of the text of Genesis, so believers of monotheistic religions can explore how Peterson's concepts can be personally useful to readers of various faiths and denominations.

Volume 4
Clean Your Room: An Out-of-the-Box Manual for Lobsters

By Annette Poizner, MSW, Ed.D., RSW

The presidential nominations are underway & Dr. Jordan Peterson nominates you . . . to take bold steps to move your life forward. Ready to turn a new leaf in 2020? Annette Poizner, a therapist, educator and author, extends Peterson's maxim 'Clean your room', making the case for lifestyle changes that may not be on your radar. Contemplating the start of a new decade, Poizner takes instruction from the first beginning on record, as it is conceived in Genesis. Can lessons embedded in that narrative speak to the contemporary lifestyle? Poizner makes the case that old wisdom, peppered with insights from Jordan Peterson, himself, will guide you toward better outcomes. Plan your New Year's Resolutions with the help of a seasoned therapist. Bring your 2020 vision into focus.

Volume 5
In Good Standing: Using Jordan Peterson's Insights on the Structure of Self to Sort Yourself Out*

By Annette Poizner, MSW, Ed.D., RSW

Your self has a structure, indirectly alluded to by Dr. Jordan Peterson each time he counsels you to live in alignment, whenever he urges you to stand with your shoulders back and every time he urges you to notice where you're aiming. Even the English

'Personal Pronoun I' alludes to that structure. Look carefully. Back 8 words. See it? It's a straight line.

Therapist Annette Poizner asserts that the archetype of the line, unpacked, delivers a myriad of lessons which can be applied to master the living of life. She will introduce the three-step pattern that underpins reality, expressed in hormonal patterns and stoplights, revealed in classic myths and modern-day acronyms, applied in building structures and hair braiding techniques. In all these, we find a trinity that sits at the root of creation, one referred to in the day-to-day vernacular as "beginning, middle and end," so naming the three points on a straight line. Watch as the contours of reality come into focus, bringing an awareness of a structure that pervades creation . . . and, more importantly, *yourself.*

Poizner, a seasoned clinician, doctoral level practitioner and certified graphologist, will pepper this presentation with references from the Hebrew Bible, other sources *and* with handwritings of prominent public figures! Turns out that we dance with the straight line each time we pick up a pen! We will meet the line in all its manifestations and befriend the archetype that grows us up, helps us stand tall, aims us forward and culminates, ideally, in a singular ego identity. We will come to see that each lie is nothing but a line with a missing piece and will understand that we spell our best success when we embrace the G-d-given archetype and, in so doing, actualize our Divine birthright. We have, after all, been lovingly made in the image of the One, the Only.

With a book designed to change your map of meaning and your perspective of life, you can take Peterson's ideas to the next level. Insights advanced by Rabbi Dr. Akiva Tatz, a Talmudic sage whose scope and intellect matches that of Peterson, will be harnessed by your guide, an author whose psychotherapy practice of 30 years compels a practical vision of what readers need to know to make meaningful and lasting life changes.

Volume 6

From Chaos to Order: A Guide to Jordan Peterson's Worldview

By Annette Poizner, MSW, Ed.D., RSW

Struggling to decipher Jordan Peterson's core worldview when you listen on YouTube? Finding that his mosaic style, fascinating tangents and detours into the mythic realm make him hard to follow? Or maybe you're wondering what the fuss is about and would like a concise introduction to Jordan Peterson's mentality, particularly as it relates to the task of sorting yourself out?

In this book, a seasoned therapist takes you on a tour of Peterson's central ideas. In a clear, linear presentation, Annette Poizner presents Peterson's premises about reality and the specific ways we perceive and organize that reality. She introduces his ideas regarding the map of meaning, outlines his take on how and why our life maps are easily corrupted and follows with his premises about the psychological necessity of the G-d ideal, tracing the sequelae when that ideal is absent, as it is in secular society. Finally, Poizner renders Peterson's map of the life space. We come to see how his rules help readers thrive in reality, given the contours of reality that he discusses. Prepare to see life from a unique, surprising and relevant vantage point.

In providing the scaffolding of Peterson's core arguments, Poizner gifts readers with a big picture that will help them when they read or listen to Peterson, facilitating better comprehension and alleviating some of the inevitable review normally required when working through his material. At the same time, this work bridges material from his two bestselling books, his Biblical lecture series and his University of Toronto courses, depicting overarching themes that emerge across platforms and presenting those clinical insights that have implications for contemporary life. Readers gain a lens through which they can consider their own personal process and are given reflection points that they can use to explore the personal relevance of ideas discussed.

Volume 7

*Yin, Yang & You: An Eastern Commentary on Jordan Peterson's 12 Rules for Life**

By Annette Poizner, MSW, Ed.D., RSW

Books that achieve bestseller status are often those that render essential truths, ideas core to our humanity. This is the case, says therapist Annette Poizner, regarding the works of Canadian psychologist Jordan Peterson. In this book, Poizner will analyze Peterson's *12 Rules for Life*, peering through the lens of Traditional Chinese Medicine's Five Element Theory in order to show how his material resonates deeply with a classic and ancient philosophical system.

Five Element Theory posits that five root elements underpin our world, our bodies and even our unique and varied psychologies. The theory renders a detailed understanding of how these elements are best choreographed to achieve a working harmony. Each element governs particular bodily systems but also relates to central psychological attributes. In *Yin, Yang & You*, we will see how Eastern truths shine out of Peterson's teachings, demonstrating why readers best heed Peterson's principles. Learn the infrastructure of your best self and clarify the choreography you can use to achieve it.

In creative chapters ('Learning How to Wok') that take readers on a tour through Peterson's worldview and Eastern premises of health, readers will learn the component parts of their psycho-spiritual constitutions and may come to recognize one particular element that constitutes their unique and personal soul root.

Readers will garner lifestyle advice that will help them in their quest to balance the inner elements. We will explore 12 as the number that represents the harmonic integration of the masculine polarity, Yang (associated with the number one) with the feminine polarity, Yin (associated with the number two). In concluding chapters, we will look at the current state of the world, the impact of the Corona virus which has painfully corrected an overriding worldwide Yang excess/imbalance, counterbalancing it with a heavy-handed Yin redress. We will use ancient Chinese wisdom to help us chart a course, as we pursue the long-lost balance. Use Peterson's wisdom in tandem with ancient Eastern principles to find your way forward in the troubling and difficult times ahead.

Due out in September, 2020.

Volume 8

Beyond Chaos: Wrestling with Jordan Peterson's Notion of the Feminine*

By Annette Poizner, MSW, Ed.D., RSW

Thousands report that Jordan Peterson's insights have helped them achieve life-altering change. Yet, by Peterson's own admission, the lion's share of his followers are male. Are there jewels in his opus which could be accessed by women? Psychotherapist Annette Poizner says there are, but first this group needs to better understand what Peterson is actually saying about the feminine. Materials needs to be prepared which will speak to the female sensibility and help dismantle the resistance that prevents some women from approaching Peterson's work.

Does Peterson's talk of 'chaos' as feminine trigger you? Do you disagree with many of his political positions? Poizner asserts that approaching his material with a will to understand yields rewards: readers can benefit from insights, ideas that usefully deviate from the usual societal narrative, while maintaining the license to reject those (political or otherwise) that don't jibe for any given woman. She asserts that women *can* benefit from the materials that Peterson has generously shared online, leveraging insights to achieve significant personal change and delving into constructs of masculine and feminine that are as old as antiquity.

Annette Poizner, a writer, therapist and executive coach, brings unique credentials to the task of introducing Peterson's opus specifically to those women who have, to date, stood in opposition. Born in the 60's, Poizner grew up an avid feminist and remains committed to progress for women. Her clinical work, steeped in Chinese medical theory, the wisdom of the ancient Kabbalah and the psychology of Carl Jung, equips her to perform a rich and detailed rendering of *Yin* and *Yang*, masculine and feminine, towards the end of unpacking Peterson's frame in a way that brings the teachings to life.

Poizner, who herself differs with Peterson on a range of issues, is working to provide a bridge for women who need help getting over the hump: helping them understand where Peterson has been vilified and misquoted, where he advances clinical insight that can be used to make life better and where they can easily agree to disagree with him. In terms of the latter, in so doing women can deliciously host the paradox of life, itself; the paradox that the masculine and feminine polarities are, more than anything else, here to teach us; the paradox, that, more than anything else, represents the central task of life, what we are here to learn.

Visit the webstore for more information: https://macrourl.com/annettestore